Dream Weavers

Textile Art from the Tibetan Plateau

Dream Weavers

Textile Art from the Tibetan Plateau

Thomas Cole

 Times Editions
Marshall Cavendish

© 2004 Marshall Cavendish International (Asia) Private Limited

Editor: Lee Mei Lin
Designers: Jailani Basari and Geoslyn Lim

Published by **Times Editions**—Marshall Cavendish
An imprint of Marshall Cavendish International (Asia) Private Limited
A member of Times Publishing Limited
Times Centre, 1 New Industrial Road, Singapore 536196
Tel: (65) 6213 9288   Fax: (65) 6285 4871
E-mail: te@sg.marshallcavendish.com
Online Bookstore: www.marshallcavendish.com/genref

Malaysian Office:
Federal Publications Sdn Berhad (General & Reference Publishing) (3024D)
Times Subang, Lot 46, Persiaran Teknologi Subang
Subang Hi-Tech Industrial Park
Batu Tiga, 40000 Shah Alam
Selangor Darul Ehsan, Malaysia
Tel: (603) 5635 2191   Fax: (603) 5635 2706
E-mail: cchong@tpg.com.my

National Library Board (Singapore) Cataloguing in Publication Data
Cole, Thomas, 1951-
Dream weavers : textile art from Tibetan plateau / Thomas Cole.—
Singapore : Times Editions, c2004.
p. cm.
Includes bibliographical references.
ISBN : 981-232-941-2
1. Rugs, Oriental—China—Tibet. 2. Rugs, Oriental—China—Tibet—
Pictorial works. I. Title.
NK2883
746.7515 — dc21   SLS2004027754

Printed and bound in Singapore by Saik Wah Press Pte. Ltd.

Photographs of rugs by Sachidhanandam T. N.

The publisher would like to thank the following for permission to reproduce photographs:
• Rosemary Jones Tung: 13, 18, 25, 33, 48 • The British Museum: 24, 41 • The British Library: 31
• The State Hermitage Museum, St. Petersburg: 45 • Thomas Cole: 35

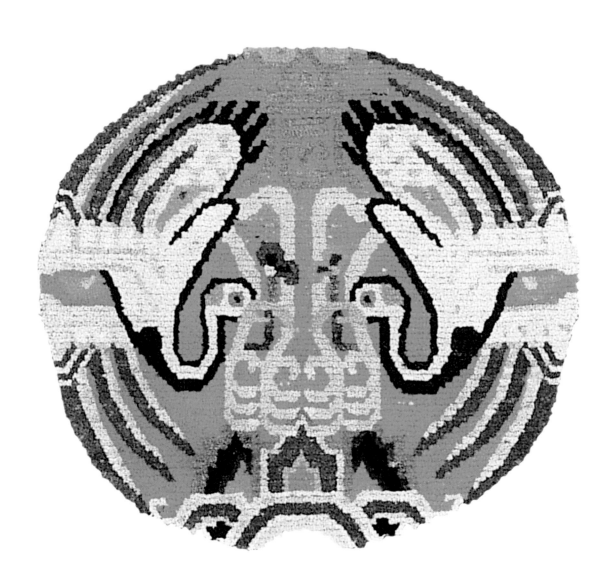

Contents

Foreword

Of the many passions life inspires, collecting art intrigues me most. My devotion to assembling a collection of Tibetan rugs began in a dark and dusty shop in Lhasa, Tibet, but my love of art has been incubating since childhood, stimulated by the beauty of Italian sculpture and cathedrals, and the land and sky of Puglia, a region of Italy where I was born and lived for many years. An intensive study of rugs and paintings in London furthered my education, yet it was a move to Singapore in 1990 that finally spurred my desire to learn more about the cultural and aesthetic traditions of Asia—a move that compelled yet another journey that was to provide access to an art form more visually rich, spiritually vibrant and intellectually satisfying than any I had previously encountered.

The memory of my first trip to Tibet remains vivid. Accompanied by my twin brother, his wife and dear friends, I flew through Hong Kong and Chengdu to Lhasa, "Land of the Gods." As the airplane approached the capital, I pressed my nose to the window, trying to get a glimpse of this remote land and its people through dramatic corridors of ice-encrusted mountains. My heart beat faster as we disembarked; not solely an effect, as one might expect, of the extremely high altitude, but rather due to the fact that I had spotted, in a car parked alongside the runway, several rugs rolled up and piled in the back. They reminded me of the Caucasian carpets I had ardently collected several years earlier, and I was immediately drawn to their bold, brilliant colors.

Our group ventured out into the city of Lhasa under a blazing azure sky. The temples, the tanned faces of the people, the colorful regional costumes and the Tibetans' reverence for their religions impressed me deeply. As we viewed the Jokhang Temple, I felt an impulse to leave the group in order to scout for rugs and soon discovered they were sold in the Barkhor, the marketplace surrounding the ancient temple. The next morning, just as the shops were opening, I moved quickly to verify that the most interesting rugs exhibited a level of craftsmanship and chromatic intelligence commensurate with the beautiful clothes, furniture and ornaments I had admired at the Potala Palace. I knew in this moment I was going to start a collection of Tibetan rugs.

Good fortune led me to a shop where the owner spoke excellent English. I was able to question him about the tradition and technique of knotting, which was totally different from what I had seen in other rug weaving cultures. He took me into a back room where hundreds of rugs were neatly stacked, and I asked if he could date, describe and explain the design and symbolism of each one. He agreed. I proceeded to spend a delightful day perusing a collection of Tibetan rugs far larger than I could have ever hoped to see in any European shop. Overwhelmed with joy despite the dust, I chose 50 rugs for serious consideration, including one with a dragon and phoenix motif set against a midnight blue ground, and another with a green and lacquer red checkerboard design. I dared not ask the prices.

The next day, I narrowed my selection down to 27 rugs—all worthy of attention in terms of beauty, design, extravagant color and exceptionally lustrous wool. Although I was able to purchase only 16 rugs, it was on that day, in a small and dusty shop, that I commenced my exhilarating journey into the world of Tibetan rugs. Since then, there is no trip I have taken anywhere in the world where I have not searched for these rugs.

Collecting old Tibetan rugs has offered me a rich experience, both visually and culturally, beyond anything I could have ever imagined. The collection has continued to grow over the years and presently numbers more than 140 rugs. Significant acquisitions in the last five years reflect the refined eye, intuitive acumen and discerning approach of Shirin De Giosa, my wife who also shares this passion. The impetus for documenting this collection belongs to her, and the birth of our nascent dream—to share our passion for this art with our friends and other Tibetan rug enthusiasts—is due, in no small part, to her vision and adamant persistence. I thank her for her invaluable support.

Shirin and I would like to take this opportunity to thank all the people who have provided us with their suggestions, advice and continuous encouragement toward the publication of this book. In particular, we would like to thank Sachi, the photographer who provided these beautiful images. We would also like to thank Helen Lim, whose dedication to this project has been vital to its success. There are many more friends who we would like to mention and personally thank; however, the list would never be exhaustive so we prefer not to name them individually. Finally, we dedicate the realization of this dream to our parents, Rosaria and Nicola, and Felicity and Francis—to whom we are eternally grateful.

Shirin and Giuseppe De Giosa

Author's Acknowledgements

I have to thank so many people who have contributed to this essay in one way or another; the list is long but necessary. First, I must thank Shirin and Giuseppe De Giosa for inviting me to write this text and for the ease with which we coordinated our collective efforts. I also wish to acknowledge Tsering Tashi and Mohan Sakya of Kathmandu, as well as Jigme-la Gyaltsen and Lok Sakya of Boudha, the dealers with whom I saw Tibetan rugs for the first time. Along with Bruce Miller, they introduced me to the life as well as the arts of the Himalayas.

I want to thank Michael Malcolm, James Allen and Alan Petrie for providing me with some of the reference books that have proven invaluable to the preparation of this text; express my gratitude to Anne Halley and Michael Craycraft for choosing to exhibit Tibetan rugs and for encouraging me to both write and speak on the subject. My appreciation also extends to Robert Pinner who has invariably supported my efforts, as well as to Arthur Leeper, Bill Liske, Tony Anninos, Rupert Smith and Thom Mond for engaging in meaningful conversation and spirited debate about the rugs, the craft and our respective interpretations.

I also wish to acknowledge and thank the editors of HALI for providing the forum for publishing my first thoughts on the subject so long ago, and I am particularly grateful to HALI's current Editor, Daniel Shaffer, whose unfailing support for this and other projects in the past has proven invaluable.

Special thanks to my two children, Katherine and Lek, for their understanding and support in the face of what must, at times, have seemed like madness.

And finally, my eternal gratitude goes to Lesley Gamble, without whom this project would have never reached fruition; I thank her for her intellectual acuity and contributions. I also thank her for inspiring me to visualize and dream about creating 'art,' and for her ardent support and assistance in traversing the gaps, both in the course of this text and in life.

Dedicated to my father, with his love and respect for the printed word.

Who are the 'Tibetans'?

*"When man made his first appearance we need not ask, but there can be
no reasonable doubt that the Tibetan is the latest survival of the
ancient Turko-Mongol stock which once prevailed through all high Asia."*[1]

In 1987, Christopher Beckwith of the University of Indiana published a book documenting
the early history of Tibet. Although largely ignored by students of Tibetan weaving, *The
Tibetan Empire in Central Asia* situates the Tibetan people and their culture within a pan-
Asian or, more specifically, Central Asian framework. Unlike the mythologizing that
characterizes much of what has been written about Tibet, Beckwith's writing, based on
historical fact, invites a thorough reassessment of the people and their culture.

Traditional perceptions of Tibetan rug production and the craft of weaving in general
were formulated without consideration of the context from which the people themselves
emerged and, as a consequence, all textile production was interpreted as a Buddhist-inspired
art form. Yet the early history of Tibet clearly portrays a people intimately related to and
involved in the broader cultural dynamics of Central Asia. In a departure from previous
scholarship, it is the premise of this book that Tibetan carpets, as a widely practiced secular
craft, reflect this dynamic.

Myth and Legend

Few legends exist and traditional speculation has not ventured beyond the accepted view
of Tibetans as members of a 'mongoloid' racial group. The primary legend recounting the
origins of the Tibetan people identifies them as the descendents of a union between a
forest monkey and a demoness who met in Yarlung, a region of Central Tibet. This
identification, however, may be more political than cultural since it is probably motivated,
as noted Tibetologists assert, "by a wish to place the nation's origins in the district where

---

1   *Tibet The Mysterious*, Sir Thomas Holdich, 35

the first kings appeared" (Stein, 28). Although Yarlung has remained the seat of Tibetan power to this day, this myth reveals little about the historical reality of the general population.

Walking around the centrally located Barkhor in Lhasa, even a casual glance at the people who are circumambulating the holy shrine of the Jokhang registers a very diverse group of people clearly composed of distinct ethnic types: the people from Amdo, who have light skin; the rugged Central Tibetans, whose features are neither Asiatic nor Mongoloid; and the Khampas of eastern Tibet, who are fairer, taller and heavier than most other Tibetans. In addition, there are always nomads or *drokpa* clustered in small groups; clad mainly in animal skins, their rough-hewn facial features and darker skin distinguish them as peoples of the steppe.

Aside from having been identified as 'nomads,' little is known of *drokpa* racial or ethnic origins. But the *drokpa* of Ladakh relate a legend that traces their ancestry back to Indo-Aryan or Indo-Scythian stock. Inhabiting a region previously known as 'Little Tibet,' they believe themselves to have migrated more than 1000 years ago from Central Asia, passing through Gilgit in northern Pakistan to settle in their present locale. Photographs published by R. Bedi in his 1981 book *Ladakh* seem to bear out these claims, depicting a people who, in dress as well as physical appearance, resemble Pashtuns more than Tibetans or Ladakhis. No similar claims or legends exist among other groups of Tibetan *drokpa*, but additional myths, interpreted and recorded by ecclesiastic scribes, were propagated later through texts claiming historical authenticity. As research from Beckwith and other scholars indicate, however, historical records do exist, requiring us to re-evaluate the ethnic origins of the Tibetan people.

The Early History of Tibet

"Early Chinese sources refer to a Tibet that was organized along tribal lines and had no effective central authority."[2]

The people believed to have exerted "a crucial formative influence on the proto-Tibetans" are the Yueh-Chih, mounted Scythian warriors who, around 200 BCE, were subjugated by the Hsiung-nu, another tribal group later known as the Huns (Beckwith, 6). The main body of the defeated Yueh-Chih fled to Central Asia and established the Kushan Dynasty in Uddiyana (Afghanistan and Pakistan). A smaller number, known as the Little Yueh-Chih, settled among the Tibetans south of the Nanshan and adopted their language.[3] These "horse-riding nomads of the north" then forged an alliance with "the sheep-driving nomads of Tibet" (Parker, 24). Together, according to ancient Chinese sources, they embarked upon a "perpetual war of raiding and cattle-lifting along the whole line of the Chinese frontier" (Parker, 24). At this point, as Markham comments, Tibet "consisted of a great variety of tribes more or less addicted to the pastoral life. At times they appear to have united into powerful confederacies and become formidable to their neighbors" (Markham, 9).

The assimilation of one tribal group by another is not unusual in Central Asia and historians of the region believe that a segment of the Yueh-Chih was absorbed into the existing native population of the plateau. While the physical isolation of the plateau itself offered a certain security from invading hordes, it also provided a safe haven or refuge for less powerful groups who had been subjugated and forced to evacuate lands they had previously occupied comfortably.

The histories of ancient Inner Asia may often appear confusing to the casual student as nomadic groups referred to by a particular name at one point in their history may

---

2   *Chinese and Exotic Rugs*, Murray Eiland, 75
3   *The Empire of the Steppes—A History of Central Asia*, René Grousset, 28–29

assume another different or loosely related identity at a later date. This apparent morphing of tribal identity and cultural homogeneity can be explained by the fact that over long periods of time, the ebbs and flows of power virtually swept some peoples out of existence. As battles were fought and the vanquished were absorbed into a conquering horde, the identity of any one group became almost impossible to discern. Tribes, customs and languages intermingled, and "slave and master lived very much in the same way, the only difference being that one did the menial work whilst the other enjoyed himself" (Parker, 10–11).

Given this complexity of tribal relationships and histories, it is possible that the people we call 'Tibetan' today may also trace their ancestry to the Tokharians.[4] Considered by many historians to be synonymous with the Yueh-Chih, the Tokharians, "well known to Greek historians," emigrated from Turkestan to Bactria in the 2nd century BCE (Grousset, 27). Textile historian Elizabeth Barber traces the Tokharians, as the "Little Yueh Chih," even farther back in time, arguing that it was they who, around 1200 BCE, practiced weaving near Hami in the Tarim Basin of present-day Xinjiang.[5] This ancestral connection to the Yueh-Chih and the textile weaving Tokharians situates the people of Tibet within a Central Asian ethno-cultural context from very early times.

Central Asian Influences on Tibetan Culture

An Empire Lost in the Mists of Time

Although the ancient Zhang Zhung civilization remains a mystery to many historians who, frustrated by the absence of a Tibetan script and tangible historical records, have relegated it to the fringe of Tibetan studies, this culture offers some important clues to

4 *The Empire of the Steppes—A History of Central Asia*, René Grousset, 27
5 *The Mummies of Urumchi*, Elizabeth Barber, 166

comprehending the influence of Central Asian culture on Tibet. For the most part, traditional scholarship has chosen to interpret the history of Tibet within a Buddhist context, ignoring the fact that the far older Zhang Zhung culture introduced Bon, the animist and shamanist pre-Buddhist religion still practiced today, into Tibet. Even though the dates, location and origin of this civilization remain largely a matter of speculation even for scholars devoted to the field, a consideration of its aesthetic and spiritual influence is essential to any discussion of Tibetan weaving.[6]

Based on texts translated from the Persian language into Zhang Zhung and Tibetan, Russian Tibetologist B. I. Kuznetsov hypothesizes that the Zhang Zhung people may have emigrated from the ancient Persian Empire sometime between 600 BCE and 200 CE. During this period, the Zhang Zhung empire was divided into three areas: inner, middle and outer. The inner area was Barzig (Persia); the middle probably occupied areas now known as Kashmir and Gilgit, extending into Ladakh and Kailash in western Tibet; while outer Zhang Zhung may have reached as far as Amdo in the extreme northeast of Tibet and the Tsaidan region of Kansu in western China. Oddly enough, the historical figure Padmasambhava, who renewed interest in Buddhism sometime in the mid-8th century, is purported to have come from the Swat Valley or Ghazni in eastern Afghanistan while Shen-rapa, the founder of modern Bon, is said to hail from the same area.[7] Given the geographic range of the Zhang Zhung empire, it is perhaps not surprising to discover significant influence from the west, in particular from the Pamir area, in the histories of Tibet's two primary religions, Buddhism and Bon.

Scholars also speculate there was a Zhang Zhung language that was identical to, or formed the basis of, Bon—one of the plateau's earliest languages. While Bon texts, according to Tibetan scholar Namkhai Norbu, do exist to this day, they are written in a script unintelligible to students of Tibetan or Sanskrit. There is a link, however, between the Zhang Zhung culture—with origins traceable to Persia—and the appearance of Persian

---

6 John Bellezza, a noted Tibetologist, has written much on this subject, tirelessly documenting early petroglyphs and rock painting on the high plateau attributable to the pre-Buddhist period and the Zhang Zhung culture.

7 This area is the part of the ancient Persian Empire that extends into Turkestan and Afghanistan and touches the Pamir region.

words in modern Tibetan. Although several early European explorers record their surprise at encountering Persian words in Tibetan locales as far removed as the traditional Bon stronghold of Amdo, their discovery is quite logical given the historical relationship between Bon religion and the Zhang Zhung empire. Significantly, the Tibetan terms for 'rug' and 'to weave' may also derive from Persian roots, clearly leaving speculation open as to the very origins of the craft itself.[8]

Assimilation: Bon and Buddhism

"The Buddhist religion, as seen in Tibetan countries has nothing in common with the pure morality preached by Gautama Buddha...bearing hardly any resemblance to the original."[9]

Buddhism was first embraced and promoted as the state religion of Tibet during the reign of the Tibetan king, Songsten Gampo (619–649 CE). The fact that it was fostered through marriages with princesses from Nepal and China may account for the pre-occupation of contemporary scholars with these particular cultures as primary sources of influence. While there is no evidence that Songsten Gampo himself was a serious practitioner of the new religion, it was during his reign that the construction of the Jokhang temple, Tibet's holiest shrine, was begun. Despite his propagation of Buddhism, however, Songsten Gampo did not neglect Bon and encouraged its co-existence with Buddhism. He even incorporated Bon myths and "traditions of the storytellers" into the wall paintings of his temple in Lhasa (Stein, 234).

Although Bon was probably brought into the plateau with the expansion of the Zhang Zhung empire, its rituals were in many ways compatible with indigenous Tibetan beliefs as both groups practiced forms of animism and shamanism that may have been quite sophisticated. "According to Bon tradition, their religion was highly advanced" and documents from Dunhuang record "funerary and propitiation rituals of great intricacy,

---

8   *Temple, Household, Horseback—Rugs of the Tibetan Plateau*, Diana Myers, 34
9   *Diary of a Journey Across Tibet*, Hamilton Bower, 13

encompassing a rich material culture. These religious traditions are far beyond our usual understanding of tribal shamanism."[10] With the increasing influence of Buddhism, however, cohabitation with Bon proved tenuous; subsequently, its practitioners were subject to banishment and exile. In spite of this, Bon continues to persist even to this day, as its animist aspects—most visible in the animal models and masked performers of Tibet's traditional ritual dances—have transformed Tibetan Buddhism into something far beyond Indian tantrism or any other form of Mahayana Buddhism.

Bonds Forged Through Marriage and Modern Statecraft

Political assimilation was a somewhat more intriguing affair. Apparently the king of Zhang Zhung and Songsten Gampo exchanged their

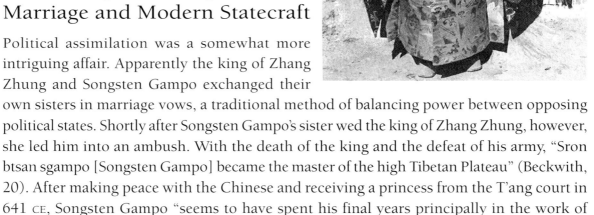

own sisters in marriage vows, a traditional method of balancing power between opposing political states. Shortly after Songsten Gampo's sister wed the king of Zhang Zhung, however, she led him into an ambush. With the death of the king and the defeat of his army, "Sron btsan sgampo [Songsten Gampo] became the master of the high Tibetan Plateau" (Beckwith, 20). After making peace with the Chinese and receiving a princess from the T'ang court in 641 CE, Songsten Gampo "seems to have spent his final years principally in the work of

---

10 Information about these documents and rituals come from noted Tibetologist John Belleza and is based upon private correspondence dated August 16, 2004.

assimilating the former Zan-zun [Zhang-Zhung] state into his empire" (Beckwith, 20). With his sudden and untimely death in 649 CE at the age of 30, authority over the kingdom effectively passed to his prime minister who continued to exert Tibet's new found power.

Occupying the conquered territory of Zhang Zhung to the west, the Tibetans subsequently allied themselves with local Turkic tribes in order to confront the armies of the Chinese T'ang Dynasty; after all, both groups had a vested interest in controlling as much of the lucrative Silk Route trade as possible. From the Khotan oasis in present-day Xinjiang, the Tibetan armies moved through the high Himalayan passes, occupied the area of Gilgit in northern Pakistan, and continued to repel numerous T'ang encroachments into Central Asia. These military alliances are not generally recognized in traditional Tibetan studies nor by scholars with an interest in carpets and textiles of the region. Given the geographic circumstances, however, it is easy to imagine opportunities for the Tibetans and the Turks to share aesthetic sensibilities, culminating in related design pools deeply rooted in Central Asian tribal traditions.

Medieval Glimpses of Tibet

Travel Accounts from the 13th through the 18th Centuries

Histories of the plateau region in the 10th to 12th centuries are incomplete, but records left behind by the Sakya or 'red hat' sect as they achieved political and ecclesiastical dominance over Tibet in the 13th century provide some insight into the Tibet of that period. From those records, the dichotomy between two contiguous cultures—the nomadic and the urban—becomes evident.

Upon their investiture as heads of the thirteen provinces of Tibet, Sakya rulers documented receiving power over the Tibetans who had "wooden doors" or *shing-sgo can* on their houses, a clarification which implies they did not obtain control over the tent-dwelling nomads.[11] In addition, population censuses held in 1268 CE and 1287 CE under the aegis of the great Khan carefully distinguish between 'Tibetans' (*Bod*) and 'nomads' (*brog*).[12] The distinction was observed again in the 1384 CE census held by the lord of Gyantse.[13] A 16th-century European account also describes the people of Tibet as divided into two primary groups: "Bolpa (Bod-pa), who live in villages and towns, and Canbah (khampas, elsewhere referred to as 'dolpah', ie 'brog-pa') who are nomads" (Stein, 110).

Europeans traveling through Tibet in the 13th and 14th centuries also recorded their impressions. Although some historians dispute the presence of western travelers at this time, the commentary of Friar Odorico, the "first [European] in the Tibetan field," is still considered reliable and significant.[14] Venturing into a kingdom subject to the Mongol ruler of China, Kublai Khan, Odorico noted that many of Tibet's inhabitants lived "in tents made of black felt" and described their principal city, Lhasa, as "surrounded with fair and beautiful walls, being built of white and black stones" (Komroff, 244). From a contemporary perspective, the people of the "tents made of black felt" probably represent a different culture or possibly a different ethnic group from those who had built Lhasa, an impressive stone city hardly compatible with nomadic sensibilities. A picturesque map

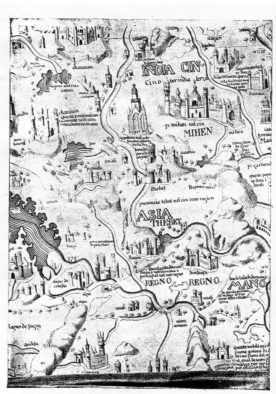

Fra Mauro's Map of Tibet, 1459

---

11 *Tibetan Civilization*, R. A. Stein, 110
12 *ibid*
13 *ibid*
14 *Tibet The Mysterious*, Sir Thomas Holdich, 70

of Tibet (facing page), drawn in 1459 and reproduced by Holdich, depicts conical dwellings that suggest round tents.[15] Curiously, these forms are reminiscent of the yurts used by the Turko-Mongol tribes of the Central Asian steppes. Although, at present, there is no evidence of this type of abode in Tibet, these representations indicate that Turko-Mongol style yurts may have, at one time, sheltered at least part of the population inhabiting the plateau.

Later travelogues compiled by European adventurers are also thought provoking. Johann Grueber's account of his early journey in 1656 CE from Peking to Lhasa is replete with references to Central Asian nomads in Tibet. Having entered what is now considered northeast Tibet, he described that part of the country as an area inhabited by a Tatar nomad group who were known to rob caravans and who settled "with their portable cities on the banks of the rivers" during particular seasons. His description of their tents constructed of "small sticks twisted or plaited together, and covered with a coarse woolen stuff bound together with cords" recalls the classic Central Asian *aul* or yurt (Markham, 297).

In the early 18th century, Francesco Orazio della Penna describes an area of northern Tibet as populated by the Hor, a nomadic warrior group who "wear their hair in tresses and dress in the Tatar fashion; they live in tents and speak both Tatar and Tibetan, but the former with greater facility" (Markham, 309–313). Penna also describes two types of tent-dwelling people: one group who live in "tents of felt" and another who reside in tents of "cloth woven out of hair" (Markham, 309–313). These different abodes indicate at least two groups of nomads living in the same area, a situation conducive to exchanges of language and culture.

---

15 Some may view the map as ambiguous and I can understand this, but the circular structures are intriguing. Buildings in this form do not exist in Tibet, either in the past or presently. Even the *stupas* in Tibet, while circular in form, are composed of foundations with squared blocks of stones. The structures retain the appearance of squares arranged in a circle rather than truly rounded as they appear in this map.

Accounts from W. W. Rockhill

No account of Tibet, historical, religious or ethnographic, would be complete without mention of William Woodville Rockhill (1854–1914), the first American to learn Tibetan and explore the plateau's innermost highlands. A meticulous scholar, respected diplomat, seasoned explorer and accomplished linguist, his translations of historical narratives by westerners traveling through the region, in addition to his own travelogue documenting journeys through China, Mongolia and Tibet, have proven invaluable to the field of Sino-Tibetan studies. Rockhill's objective was to provide historical, ethnographic and geographic documentation of the country. While much of his research was conducted during the four years he resided in Peking enjoying "daily and intimate intercourses with natives from various parts of Tibet and the borderlands of Kan-su," it is his first-hand observations that provoke questions and provide clues relevant to Tibet's ethnic and, by association, textile histories (Rockhill, Preface).

Traveling through eastern Tibet, Rockhill encountered a group of Salor Turkmen who had no written history of their migration but maintained that their advent dated from about the middle of the 14th century (Holdich, 176–177). They continued to speak their native Turkmen dialect which, "perfectly intelligible" to the traders of Xinjiang, indicated that they could still communicate with peoples native to their original homeland of Turkestan.[16] Given the documented presence of these accomplished Turkic weavers inhabiting Tibet for perhaps the last 600 years, we might wonder if their weaving practices have influenced the Tibetans. We do know that this influence extended to at least as far as their tribal neighbors, the Kargan, who had converted to Islam, the religion of the Turkic groups. And when some of Rockhill's group consulted a famous fortune-teller in Kam, Rockhill recalled that the sorcerers of the Uighers, a Turkic people neighboring Tibet, were also called Kham, leading him to speculate that the Tibetan Kham oracle may have descended from ancient Turkic stock.

---

16 *The Land of the Lamas*, W. W. Rockhill, 40

Given the complexity of Tibetan history and its multi-ethnic components, the parameter of Tibetan identity has often been defined by language use; in other words, people who use the Tibetan language are classified as Tibetan. But the adoption of a language or, by association, the loss of a mother tongue, does not alter ethnic origins or the distant memories of specific traditions practiced in a tribal past. Rockhill's observations inevitably suggest that the people who have been grouped together under the all-inclusive term 'Tibetan' are multi-ethnic and tribal, prompting the necessity to re-evaluate our understanding of who may have actually woven those rugs referred to as 'Tibetan'.

Origins of the Craft

Given the harsh environment that dominates most areas within the political boundaries of Tibet, the production of pile weavings, while a luxury on one hand, was considered a necessity by those who were able to engage in such activities. Not all the ethnic or tribal groups in Tibet grasped the technique of pile weaving even though the practice was considered a "ubiquitous folk art."[17] The fact that it developed as a technology for domestic use rather than urban or commercial enterprise suggests the craft is old, and we do know that "weaving of some sort probably extends back as far as one can chart human habitation of the Tibetan plateau" since clay spindle whorls are often found at Neolithic sites in Tibet (Myers, 21).

Circumstantial evidence indicating an early date for Tibetan pile weaving may be found in translations of the classic biography of Milarepa, an 11th-century poet and saint whose teacher is described as being seated "on top of two layers of bolster and a carpet [*grum-tse*], making three layers with cushions, over a floor carpet [*sa-gden*]" (Myers, 26). This tradition persists even to this day, as great teachers or lamas are still seated on layers of rugs. While it is possible that these 11th-century textiles were not made in Tibet, the

---

17 *Tibetan Rugs*, Hallvard Kåre Kuløy, 27

fact that the terms '*grum-tse*' and '*sa-gden*' are still used to identify Tibetan rug types tips the evidence to support Tibetan pile weaving and a continuity of tradition spanning almost 1000 years.

At one point, Tibetan rug scholarship focused on the absence of clearly old rugs made prior to the 19th century, leading researchers to speculate that pile carpet weaving was introduced relatively recently in Tibet. While this may be possible, it is a theory that is difficult to believe since the looping method of pile weaving, which is how most Tibetan rugs are woven, is an archaic technique documented in Central Asian and Egyptian rugs

well over a thousand years old.[18] Some Central Asian fragments (shown right) unearthed by Sir Aurel Stein and dated to the 3rd and 4th centuries CE are apparently woven in this manner, as are some Egyptian or north African weavings from the 6th to 8th centuries, but the technique disappeared long ago in these particular areas.[19] Whether or not the Tibetans were influenced by these earlier textiles or simply 're-invented' this archaic method of weaving independently is difficult to ascertain. Given the probability for both a long history of weaving and the influence of Central Asian traditions on the plateau, it seems more likely that the looping technique was adopted early on. Yet the

---

18 *Frozen Tombs of Siberia—The Pazyryk Burials of Iron Age Horsemen*, Sergei Rudenko, 134, 204 Some fragmented textiles from Pazyryk indicate the use of the cut loop weaving technique, though Barber asserts in a private communication dated July 2, 2004 that many of the excavated textiles have deteriorated to the point that it is difficult to determine if the loops are actually cut or merely worn away.
19 *The Oriental Carpet*, Volkmar Gantzhorn, 74

survival of this extremely archaic method solely in Tibet remains a mystery, due, possibly, to Tibet's isolation as a theocratic Buddhist state as well as its formidable physical barriers. Since ancient times, the Tibetan state exerted power beyond its political/ethnic borders but rarely experienced forceful entries from outside, the notable exceptions being the Younghusband expedition in 1904 and, most recently, Chinese occupation since the mid-20th century.

Attribution

19th and 20th Century Observations

The historical perception of Tibet as a homogenous Buddhist society was rendered completely obsolete by the end of the 19th century but has persisted in later studies of Tibetan weaving which have inaccurately assigned a Buddhist inspiration to the tradition. A closer examination of documented sources, however, reveals that Tibetan rug weaving was rarely patronized and certainly not sponsored by the monastic communities until the late 19th century, indicating a truly secular art form.

Tibetan rugs were originally made by people for their own use. They incorporated the design pool of the steppes, which suggests an inspiration derived from a Turko-Mongol horde ancestry that pre-dates the introduction of Buddhism into Tibet. By the close of the 19th century, however, a different aesthetic—one that was developed in urban workshop environments—became popular and persisted into the

20th century. Influenced by Chinese textiles and Buddhist art as well as the design pool of northern Chinese pile weaving, these rugs do incorporate a wide range of Buddhist iconography but are devoid of the austere elegance of earlier rural and village examples.

An extremely relevant source on the subject of Tibetan weaving is the travelogue of Sarat Chandra Das (1849–1917), edited and annotated by Rockhill. Born a Hindu but later an adherent of Tibetan Buddhism, Das established relationships with Tibetan lamas in Sikkim when he traveled through the region in the late 19th century. He should be considered one of the first collectors of Tibetan rugs since, if the asking price was not too high, he acquired rugs for himself and carefully documented what he saw.[20] Contributing much to our understanding of both the geography and ethnography of Tibet, his meticulously recorded comments have proven very useful for classifying the different types of pile weavings he observed.

On one occasion, circa 1885, his description of the gifts offered to a government minister, which included blankets, Tibetan serge (*pulo*) and "Gyantse rugs of superior quality [and] Khamba rugs," defines a distinction between urban workshop and indigenous tribal production (Das, 100). Not surprisingly, given the fashion of the time, Das praises the workshop production of Gyantse, but he also recognizes the tribal 'Khamba' weavings and correctly classifies them as such. His subsequent descriptions of the Khambas (*sic.* Khampas) as "a dangerous class" and a "fierce race who infest the solitudes of Tibet and generally carry on depredations on the isolated villages north of Lhasa" imply that he was cognizant not only of the distinctions between the weavings of the various groups but also their nomadic versus sedentary lifestyles (Das, 107). Unfortunately, he never bequeathed his textile collection to any institution; only his words have been preserved for posterity.

---

20 *Journey to Lhasa and Central Tibet*, Sarat Chandra Das, 41

Nomadic (Tribal) Production?

"Among the nomad, the carpet is not a luxury;
it is a necessity which the rich and poor alike cannot do without."[21]

Several authors have undertaken the task of identifying specific tribes in Tibet: Brooke Dolan and Ilya Tolstoy identify seven groups of *drokpa* (nomads) by name; Tibetan writer Tseh-ring-thar refers to 25 tribes in the Amdo area of northeast Tibet; and Rockhill lists names for more than 50 tribes inhabiting the regions of east Tibet.[22] How important are these tribal affiliations today? The answer is unclear but a more pertinent question might be: how important were they in the 19th century and before? Life in 20th-century Tibet, as in many Central Asian cultures, has contributed to obscuring tribal identities. In the past, though, these associations were probably very meaningful.

In spite of the absence of official documentation, nomadic production in Tibet is implied in a number of first-hand accounts. In the mid-1920s, Rinchen Lhamo, a Tibetan woman married to an English civil servant stationed on the plateau, wrote: "The drokpa will have his cooking utensils, various churns and buckets, saddlery, rugs, leather bags and so on. The various properties will be neatly stacked to divide the tent into two or more recesses wherein the family sit and sleep on thick rugs spread on the ground" (Lhamo, 86). Charles Bell relates an almost identical description of the nomadic habitat: "Along the walls, or stacked so as to form recesses, we shall find our friend's daily needs: cooking utensils, buckets and churns, rugs, saddles, and leather bags containing food" (Bell, 20). Bell subsequently adds: "Others will stay in and around the tents, making the butter and cheese, spinning and weaving wool, collecting yak-dung for fuel" (Bell, 28). The clarity of both accounts regarding an established tradition for the use of rugs and Lhamo's observation

---

21 *Carpets of Central Asia*, A. A. Bogolyubov, 15 The author was a Russian military officer in the late 19th century during his sojourn in what is now Turkmenistan. Even though he was writing about the Turkmen, his comments ring true for nomads throughout Central Asia.
22 *The Ancient Zhang-Zhung Civilization*, Tseh-ring-thar, 131

of coarse, thick sleeping rugs suggest the possibility that these people were weaving rugs in addition to cloth.

Phillip Denwood of the University of London also records the nomads' use of rugs but identifies important differences: "Carpets of some sort will also be found inside the nomad's tent, as they are a convenient, transportable bedding. Those in the poorer tents may be coarse and rough, but the wealthier nomads will use the finest carpets" (Denwood, 11). The "coarse" carpets to which he refers may very well be the "thick rugs" noted by Rinchen Lhamo, a nomadic product subsequently dubbed 'warp faced back' rugs.[23] These rustic rugs are regarded by the Tibetans themselves as the earliest weaving style, situating the origin of the craft within a period when pastoral weavers engaged in the types of weaving from which the later, polished style is derived. The primitive aesthetic of the 'tsutruk' and warp faced back rugs is reminiscent of a related style and aesthetic practiced among other nomadic/tribal groups located farther to the west in Turkestan.

PLATES 57, 58
PLATES 19, 20

Traditional Tibetan rug scholarship has eschewed the premise of nomadic or tribal rug production in Tibet, but a clear definition of 'nomadic life' has not been fully articulated. All too often the term 'nomadic' is characterized by romanticized visions of nomads wandering without any established base. The reality of most nomadic groups, however, is that one part of the family, clan or tribe is engaged in pastoral or 'vertical' nomadism, moving from lowland to upland pastures and back down again in rhythm with the seasons, while the rest of the family members remain in one place, either in stationary tents or even small villages, and perform agricultural activities. This lifestyle, synchronized with conditions in the highlands of Tibet, is also conducive to rug weaving. The result is a clearly Tibetan aesthetic—a 'plateau style'—articulated in many of the rugs of this collection. Circular nomadism or perpetual migration, practices unfavourable to the somewhat sedentary work of pile weaving, are rarely practiced in Central Asia or Tibet.

---

23 This term, which refers to Tibetan weavings of a distinctive structure, first appeared in print in *A Tribal Tradition*, HALI #49, Jan/Feb 1991, Thomas Cole. Often referred to as 'Wangden' rugs in the current marketplace, this term applies to a specific village of the same name. These rugs display a variety of structural materials and diverse palettes, suggesting different provenance or places of origin. To use the term 'Wangden' as a general reference is a misnomer and may be misleading.

Provenance

During the mid-1980s, as old Tibetan rugs first began to appear in great quantity in Nepal, participants in the marketplace assigned Rockhill's name to a specific type of medallion design based on his acquisition of a particular textile now housed in the Smithsonian Institute.[24] Acquired in Kham in the mid-1880s, the rug was reputed to come from Shigatse. Unfortunately, Rockhill failed to record the exact circumstances of its acquisition, and while we may assume that Shigatse was indeed the original market for this rug, its rustic structural qualities, coarse knotting (26 kpsi), simple design and limited color scheme indicate that Shigatse was not the actual location of its production. More likely, it was woven in a smaller village.

Centers of Tibetan weaving in the late 19th century include Gyantse, renowned as a workshop center, as well as Lhasa, the seat of government and home to a wealthy urban class. The primary and most active area for high quality carpet weaving, however, "was undoubtedly the southern province of Tsang."[25] With its heavy population, relative prosperity and sheep "famed for their high quality wool," Tsang was particularly "well known for its woolen broadcloths and serges" (Denwood, 15). Specific villages of the region, such as Khampa Dzong and Wangden, provide a reference point for certain types of rugs exhibiting specific design or structural characteristics familiar to many collectors of the craft. The weavings of Khampa Dzong, often represented in early 20th-century photographs, consist primarily of sparsely patterned rugs while the village name of Wangden is loosely associated with all the "coarse and thick" rugs made in the warp faced back technique.[26]

Given the data presently available, attempts to locate the exact origins of these rugs or to identify which specific tribal groups or peoples may have woven which types of rugs are unrealistic. Further research correlating structural data (identifying specific types of

---

24 *Temple, Household, Horseback—Rugs of the Tibetan Plateau*, Diana Myers, 36
25 *The Tibetan Carpet*, Philip Denwood, 13
26 Identifying all rugs of the warp faced structural type by this name (to which Wangden refers) is akin to attributing all finely woven Tekke Turkmen rugs to Bokhara, a common marketplace misnomer promoted in the eastern marketplaces which became commonly used among buyers in the west.

wool with certain regions of Tibet), laboratory dye analyses (certain natural dyes may be indigenous to a specific area of the country) and ethnographic information (pertinent to weaving) will be necessary in order to clarify lingering questions of precise attribution and provenance. At present, however, given the dearth of scholarship in this area, suffice it to say that historical accounts do seem to correspond with the tangible evidence the rugs themselves present.

Technique

The cut or Senneh loop technique used in Tibetan weavings is a very simple yet extremely versatile technique for producing pile weavings (Fig. 1). Although this linear process is not conducive to executing curvilinear designs, Tibetan artisans ingeniously adapted the weave to include half knots, diagonal knots and even transverse knotting, where knots are

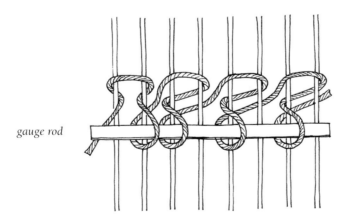

gauge rod

Fig. 1 In the Senneh loop technique, "the yarn is brought over the gauge rod and then is woven back into the carpet under the next two warps. The pile is formed by cutting the loops that remain when the gauge rod is removed." (Eiland, Chinese and Exotic Rugs, 83)

attached to adjacent wefts instead of warps. Consequently, odd structural details are common and despite the relatively coarse knot count of most old Tibetan rugs, the complexity of patterns achieved can be quite extraordinary. Unlike other weaving cultures in Central Asia, the Tibetan aesthetic is not based on any strictly codified forms, resulting in rugs with whimsically imaginative designs and, in older examples, a fluid, free hand drawing.

The vast majority of Tibetan rugs are woven on vertical looms rather than the horizontal looms employed in other Central Asian weaving cultures. Typically, vertical looms are used in village and organized factory production, while the use of horizontal looms suggests sedentary or semi-nomadic weavers. Although the Tibetans' use of vertical looms might appear to mitigate against a nomadic origin for the craft, some authors have described these looms as easy to disassemble, transport and reassemble without disturbing unfinished weaving.[27] While this portability suggests, at the very least, a potential complicity with nomadic lifestyles, more PLATES 57, 58 convincing is the fact that Tibetan 'tsutruk' rugs, as well as some related flat weaves, are made on small horizontal back strap looms. Given their very rustic appearance, these textiles may represent what is possibly the original format for pile weaving on the plateau, implying that Tibetans may have used the horizontal loom from earliest times.

---

27 *The Tibetan Carpet*, Philip Denwood, 29

Dyes

The distinctively colorful palette seen in most Tibetan weavings reflects the dyestuffs available as well as the desire of the weavers to brighten their surroundings. As in many other Central Asian weaving cultures, the drab brown landscape is oppressive and the delight people take in producing, using and looking at weavings with color cannot be discounted.

Tibetans were never renowned as master dyers and the process was generally regarded as a simple village craft. At times, extraordinary shades of deep red and aubergine, a clear yellow, a lovely green and a saturated indigo blue were achieved but with varying degrees of success. During the 1840s, immigrant dyers from Bhutan, known as Peboun, were active in the capital. Creating "vivid and enduring" colors, they were considered the master dyers of Lhasa (Huc, 182). Unfortunately, few of the rugs that testify to the art of the Peboun still exist, but the dyers of other urban workshops in Lhoka and Gyantse were also noted for their "particular skill," producing a very saturated palette with beautiful clear hues.[28]

Given the relatively harsh and inhospitable environs of the plateau region, it was often the *drokpa* or nomads who gathered dyestuffs for the sedentary dyers and weavers of Tibet. Das, who was fluent in Tibetan and quite learned in matters pertaining to the flora and fauna of the Tibetan countryside, records that the *drokpa* collected the *tso* or dye plant which "supplied a beautiful yellow color" (Das, 213). Kuløy refers to this same plant as a source for red and equates it with the madder root, but this may be an error in identification or transliterated terminology. Madder root, a traditional source for red hues, was found throughout the plateau. Given the multiple shades of red, orange, maroon and aubergine expressed in Tibetan rugs, it is probable that divergent varieties of the root existed or that dyers knew how to exploit the varying age of the root to create the desired shades.

Kuløy also identifies a number of other plants which yielded dyes; these include tumeric and safflower to produce orange; a thorny bush called *martesma* to yield pink

---

28 *Temple, Household, Horseback—Rugs of the Tibetan Plateau*, Diana Myers, 47

(although watered down madder root also serves for this color); *chutsa*, the root of a high altitude wild rhubarb plant, for yellow; barberry and tumeric plants also for yellow; and tea and walnut husks, which yield shades of brown. Indigo, imported from India and China, was available to all the dyers of the plateau, but the expertise with which this dye was handled varied. Logwood, a fugitive red dye encountered more commonly in Chinese rugs but also found in a few Tibetan rugs, fades to a shade of yellow—a planned aesthetic in Ningshia weavings but met with mixed results in Tibetan rugs. Insect based dyes such as cochineal were not indigenous to the high plateau, but lac from Bhutan was imported and used with great success to achieve light aubergine and pale red hues.

Synthetic dyes were imported into Tibet toward the end of the 19th century, making their appearance in Tibet later than in other Central Asian weaving cultures. Consistent with the history of their introduction elsewhere, madder (rubia) was the first dyestuff to be replaced by a synthetic counterpart. The difficulty of preparing a true red from rubia provided the excuse for finding a reasonable substitute. Later Tibetan weavings often include synthetic reds and pinks, while other natural dyes continued to be used into the 1940s. Mordents were gathered from various natural materials found along the banks of rivers and other bodies of water. The most commonly used mordents were "borax, common soda, alum, and copper sulphate" (Myers, 47).

PLATE 12

An interesting feature of some Tibetan rugs is the use of multi-colored yarns, plied together to achieve a 'speckled' effect. This aesthetic is unique to Tibetan rugs, another tribute to the artistic ingenuity of the weavers.

Rug Types and Functions

Used for both utilitarian and decorative purposes, Tibetan weavings appear in a staggering number of different shapes, sizes and designs—a feature that collectors find both provocative and appealing.

Rugs for Sleeping

Tibetans rarely if ever use rugs on the floors; instead, they choose to place straw mats or some other plain, undecorated material under their feet. Rugs are used primarily for sleeping and sitting. The most common type, *khaden*, is typically small, measuring approximately 3 feet by 5 feet or less. Placed on top of divans or platforms, they serve as seating during the day and bedding at night. Often, even in the homes of simple people, more than one rug is used on the sleeping platform to facilitate the preservation of those placed underneath. Floor rugs of greater size or *sa-gden* were woven as special orders in estate-sponsored workshops. Although very rare until the late 19th century, these rugs were not unknown in earlier times since they are referenced in the 14th-century biography of Milarepa.[29]

Seating Rugs for Lamas and Special Occasions

Tibetan tradition involves greeting special guests by offering them a square mat to sit upon. Described in a previous section as the textile used by Milarepa's teacher, these mats are typically 3 feet square or less and are placed on top of other rugs or bolsters. In the monasteries, monks sit in rows on runners, while small square mats are placed at the head of a long monastic rug to denote the place where an important lama will seat himself. Dubbed as 'meditation mats' in the marketplace, it is more likely many rugs of this size are simply mats on which to sit, rather than meditate.

---

29 *Temple, Household, Horseback—Rugs of the Tibetan Plateau*, Diana Myers, 26

Door Rugs

Like other Central Asian cultures, most notably the Turkmen, Tibetans cover their doors with textiles. Simply decorated, often with a flower motif symbolizing fertility, the Tibetan door cover (shown right) never exhibits the intricate iconography of a Turkmen cover or *ensi*, but both types exhibit a quartered field design with a separate skirt or valence running across one end, suggesting, once again, the probability of a shared tradition.

Tiger Rugs

"At the farther end of an apartment," the French travelers Huc and Gabet note, "we perceived a personage sitting with crossed legs on a thick cushion covered with a tiger's skin; it was the Regent" (Huc, 209). The use of tiger skins is documented, and they are usually found in the possession of physically imposing, socially prestigious or economically powerful men. Although Tibetans often chose to use a woven rather than authentic pelt, clearly they desired to retain the powerful symbolism of sitting upon or, by extension, vanquishing such an imposing beast. While the use of pelts is known throughout Central Asia, Tibetans are the only group whose weavers designed rugs patterned on these hides. This pattern does exist in some Chinese weavings, but these were made for export to the lamaist market rather than for indigenous use. Despite the fact that conventional wisdom associates the monastic community with the use of tiger rugs, the vast majority have a brown, presumably walnut-dyed ground rather than the typical ecclesiastic palette of red, maroon and orange. Though typically woven in the *khaden* format, square pieces are also known and, most likely, the vast majority of them were woven for seating special personages.

Rugs for Monastic Use

As the economic affluence of the monastic communities increased, so did their patronage of the arts. Monasteries usually commissioned rugs and textiles for their own use. In addition to buying and possibly trading for them, the monasteries also accepted rugs as tribute from adherents to the east, often in the form of lamas' throne backs and large pillar rugs.

Runners – These rugs are found in the halls of the monasteries and cover the long benches or places for seating monks. Here the monks perform *puja*, rituals consisting of the recitation of Buddhist scriptures accompanied by the ethereal sounds of drums, reverberating long horns and guttural chanting.

Runners display various designs but generally depict medallions, the motifs that designate the place where each monk will sit. Rugs of the warp faced back type—the thick, coarsely woven rugs that appear to bear a strong structural similarity to the *julhkhyrs* or bearskin rugs of the Uzbek and Kirghiz from Turkestan—are often found in these monasteries. Previously unrecognized, except for one small square mat or *khangama* in the McCoy Jones Collection,[30] these rugs became known only after they appeared in the marketplace in the late 1980s. The designs include round medallions, stepped polygon motifs, swastikas and, more commonly, concentric squares which recall the *gabbeh* aesthetic of Persian tribal weavings. These rustic textiles, woven in a village or semi-nomadic environment, may have been commissioned by the monastic communities or offered as tribute. Runners woven in more familiar techniques, unlike examples made in the archaic warp faced back structure, were probably often woven in workshops located within or adjacent to the monastic compounds.

Lamas rugs – Special weavings, often found in pairs or a set, were made for the use of high lamas and consist of a square mat connected to a triangular-shaped backrest. Chinese

---

30 photo, *A Tribal Tradition*, Thomas Cole, HALI #49, 21

Ningshia rugs were often imported for this purpose, but indigenous weavings emulating the Chinese models were also made, though less often. These rugs are truly special and often depict dragons, a symbol of power, as well as Buddhist design elements. Occasionally, weavings were made for a very specific purpose, such as covers for *dorje* bells, drums and other instruments used in the *puja* and other religious ceremonies.[31]

Pillar carpets – The cavernous halls inside the monasteries of Tibet are supported by huge pillars around which large pillar rugs are occasionally wrapped. Typically depicting the imperial dragons of the Ningshia production rugs of northern China, pillar rugs also display idiosyncratic features such as Tibetan script identifying the donor and recipient, which impart a distinctly Tibetan aesthetic. Occasionally small rugs, often referred to as 'miniature pillar rugs,' are made by sewing along the selvedges to form a cylinder and stuffing the form with straw to hold its shape. They were never intended to simulate pillars but, rather, prayer wheels. As the large prayer wheels which flank the monastery door are turned by the faithful sending prayers to the gods, these small talismanic rugs, which are adorned with abstract tiger stripes, serve to protect all who enter.

Saddlery

Saddle rugs – The horse culture of the Central Asian steppes is one that exists in parts of Tibet as well. Mounted warriors were feted in special ceremonies and competed on festive occasions such as the Monlam Festival.[32] Naturally, saddle rugs developed as both necessary and decorative accessories, their first appearance pre-dating the arrival of the decorative horse covers. Kuloy identified the earliest prototypes, which exhibit a nascent 19th-century aesthetic. They include specific design variants (Refer Kuløy, Plates 165, 173) and an archaic oval shape (Kuløy, Plates 153, 162). The more common shape is that of a rectangle

---

31 photo, *Tibetan Rugs—Chinese But With a Difference*, Nicholas Wright, Oriental Rug Review, Vol 9, #4, 10, Fig. 5
32 Extensive descriptions as well as photographs of the festivities surrounding the Monlam Festival in Lhasa appear in *A Portrait of Lost Tibet*, Rosemary Jones Tung.

with notches in two opposite corners. The 'butterfly' shape seen in later saddle rugs is PLATE 59 thought to be derived from a British prototype, introduced subsequent to the Younghusband expedition in 1904 and never seen in earlier pieces.

Horse covers – These larger weavings are very unusual and were probably made exclusively for the upper classes and special occasions. The extravagantly ornate designs suggest the PLATES 63, 64, 65, 66, 67 high esteem in which they were held. Apparently a specially commissioned workshop production, the designs are unique; every example is different, reflecting the whims of the weaver and possibly those of the sponsor. Truly old examples of this type of weaving are very rare and the vast majority exhibit characteristics of the more prolific period at the end of the 19th century and later.

Trappings – Small pile trappings for horses and mules are unusual and often exhibit some of the most truly individualized and unique patterns encountered in Tibetan weaving. The forehead trappings (*thap-gya*) used on the lead animal of a pack train are intriguing, mimicking the silhouette of an animal head, possibly a goat or ram. Decorated with a variety of ornaments, including Buddhist symbols and other secular patterns (such as flowers, tiger stripes, etc.), they are used as talismans to ensure the safety of the animal. Pile bands from which a bell might be attached are also made; these are often designed to encircle the neck of an animal. These weavings are composed of symbols that are usually simple and geometric, and rarely feature pictorial or Buddhist inspired patterns. Flat woven trappings of similar function are also found with geometric patterning. Pile weavings are also made for the rump of the horse (*s'ar*); they are attached to rear of the saddle, fanning out behind and connected under the tail of the animal.

Dating

Over the years, the parameters for accurately identifying older rugs from the plateau have become more clearly defined and understood. In 1974, Phillip Denwood characterized the older aesthetic as coarsely woven, composed of simple color schemes using natural dyes and displaying "non-representational design with borders—mostly medallion designs" (Denwood, 74). With few exceptions, older rugs maintain consistent structural characteristics with the exclusive use of wool warps and wefts in addition to woolen yarns for the pile. The use of cotton in the foundation, indicated by mill spun cotton threads, is apparently a later feature associated with the end of the 19th century. This affluent renaissance period spawned representational designs as well. Synthetic dyes were also introduced at this time, a period of increasing trade with foreign lands, primarily India.

Examining the integrity of design as a means to date Tibetan weavings is subjective and hardly definitive. The conservative nature of the craft encouraged adherence to practiced motifs; therefore, the degeneration of design was very gradual, unlike other weaving cultures where demands from foreign markets encouraged the abandonment of traditional patterns and a rapid decline in aesthetic quality. Identifying a first period (pre-1800) Tibetan weaving is difficult and speculative due to conservative stylistics and an absence of hard documentation although Murray Eiland, acknowledging the inherent danger, has offered dates on several pieces.[33] Mid-19th century rugs, woven prior to the popularization of the craft through wealthy sponsors, are generally identified using Denwood's parameters. Closer examination, however, belies his characterization of the older examples as containing a "few natural dyes" (Denwood, 75). While the palette of these earlier weavings is apparently subdued, a closer examination and the identification of specific colors by name usually reveals a more subtle and diverse palette than initially thought. Identifying rugs from the later, more prolific period of Tibetan weaving (circa 1885–1920) is more straightforward as the use of synthetic dyes and foreign materials offers a more reliable method than evaluating design.

---

33 *Tibetan Rugs at Adraskand*, Murray Eiland, Oriental Rug Review, Vol. 11, #6

Designs

The design pool of Tibetan weavings is not one that can be easily classified or compartmentalized. Attempting to identify the patterns and designs in these rugs as representative of a distinct aesthetic is not a simple exercise since myriad influences from the neighboring lands of Turkestan, Mongolia and China have created a virtual melting pot of themes and ornaments.

Chinese Silk Textile Patterns

Facsimiles of Chinese silk textile designs may be seen in some very ornate Tibetan rug designs whose dates correspond to the Yuan (1276–1368), Ming (1368–1644) and Qing (1644–1911) periods. The manner in which these rugs re-create the detailed and distinctive drawing of the silk weaving is spectacular, with particularly skilled renditions of the dragon/phoenix designs. The dragon, a primary component of local mythology throughout Asia, often represents the power of regenerative waters and the Emperor, while the phoenix is generally regarded a talisman against "illness, accident and misfortune" (Myers, 43). Though in some contexts, Chinese mythology sometimes equates the phoenix with the Empress and drought,[34] and in others with buried treasure, felicity and fire,[35] the juxtaposition of the dragon and phoenix reflects a long tradition of symbolizing opposing forces such as yin and yang, male and female, and sky and earth. Typically described as portraying 'combat,' it may be more appropriate to consider the two beasts as 'cavorting in the heavens,'[36] as displaying the potentially deadly yet fertile engagement of oppositional energies in the elegance of one stroke.

PLATE 4

Simpler brocade patterns consisting of roundels also entered the design pool of Tibetan pile weaving but, due to the use of natural dyes and the fact that these patterns have not changed much over time, dating these rugs on the basis of design alone is very difficult.

PLATES 38, 39, 40, 41

34 *Chinese Mythology*, Anthony Christie, 36
35 *Chinese Mythology*, Anthony Christie, 42, 58
36 *The Central Asian Dimension of the Symbolic System in Bactria and Margiana*, H. P. Frankfort, 411

Checkerboard

PLATES 28, 29
30, 31, 32

Rug patterns composed of abstract checkerboard and cross/check motifs are some of the most archaic in the design pool, and may be representative of a primitive talismanic aesthetic since crosses, in Tibetan culture, are used as symbols to ward off the evil eye and ensure good luck. Due to the absence of ornate patterning, critics used to speculate that student weavers produced these rugs, but this seems unlikely given the fine materials and exquisite dyes with which they are often made. Surprisingly, a 7th-century Central Asian wood panel (shown right) unearthed by Sir Aurel Stein depicts a 3-headed deity seated upon a multi-colored checkerboard textile or weaving that looks strikingly similar to the tri-colored checkerboard rugs and textiles of 19th-century Tibet. Moreover, the deity represented is supposedly the one whom the weavers of Khotan had chosen as their patron.[37] This similarity of design raises, once again, the possibility not only of a shared aesthetic but also a continuity of tradition, linking Tibetan and Central Asian weavers for more than a millennium.

PLATE 33

Related to the cross/checkerboard, the 'tigma' pattern is another essential component of textile design from the plateau. Using a tie-dye technique, it is often executed on a simple hand-woven woolen twill textile called a *poulou*. Rarely seen in the medium of pile weaving, the tigma design in Plate 33 is an extremely unusual example of the type.

---

37 *Ancient Arts of Central Asia*, Tamara Talbot Rice, 204 This painted panel dates from the period during which Tibet exerted influence in this region of Central Asia.

Tiger Motifs and Other Animal Imagery

Zoomorphic depictions are sometimes found in the Tibetan design pool and the snow lion, an image beloved by all Tibetans, is prominently featured. The pairing of these mythical beasts on the Tibetan national flag is thought to symbolize the union of the secular and religious aspects of the country. The *garuda*, a mythical bird serving as the mount for Vishnu, the four-armed Hindu god, is also occasionally rendered.

PLATE 3

Tiger motifs are depicted on some of the more interesting rugs and represent a long tradition of using animal pelts, or, in the case of Tibetans, facsimiles thereof. The market popularity of these rugs has been unparalleled and they have appeared in sufficient numbers over the years to form a critical mass from which we can view the group with perspective. A variation of this pattern places traditional medallion designs against a brown tiger stripe ground, combining the roundel design found on silk brocades with animal pelt iconography. The confluence of these designs may represent the fundamental play of the world, the imbrication of dichotomous aspects such as yin and yang.

PLATE 55

While presumably unique motifs do occur within the Tibetan design pool, they are often composed of familiar elements combined in an innovative manner. A pair of audience rugs may reflect an ancient aesthetic, as what appears to be a lion is rendered in a manner reminiscent of the 'twisted animal' style of the Scythians and yet is placed within a flaming Sassanian roundel.[38] Since no other rugs of this design type have surfaced over the years, the always-dangerous use of the word 'unique' may, in fact, be appropriate in this case.

Pre-Buddhist and Buddhist Symbols

Buddhist influences on Tibetan design emerged in the late 19th century and rarely, if ever, pre-date this period. The swastika and endless knot motifs could be exceptions, however, since both pre-date Buddhism, sharing far more achaic origins and, perhaps, a common introduction into Tibet through the older Zhang Zhung culture. The swastika in particular

---

38 refer *In The Plateau Style*, Thomas Cole, HALI #131, 78

is of great interest. Representing a spinning cross, which is also considered a talisman, its origins may be found, as some authors speculate, in celestial symbolism. We need only imagine the center of the swastika as the North Star, the focal point of the heavens, and the extended arms of the cross as constellations spinning around this central axis. Appearing as early as 5500 BCE on Anatolian pottery as well as on Central Asian BMAC (Bactria Margiana Archaeological Complex) seals dating from approximately 4000 BCE to 3000 BCE, the swastika has continued to be a motif of primary significance in both Buddhist and Hindu religious iconography to the present day.[39]

PLATES 9, 25 The use of the swastika to create a fretwork pattern is an interesting phenomenon; although difficult to weave, its eye-dazzling effects inspire weavers and viewers alike. Used as a repeating pattern in the borders of some Tibetan rugs, it may also be found in Chinese weavings as well as carpets from East Turkestan.

The endless knot (Fig. 2) is another design commonly associated with Buddhist iconography. Commonly used as a supplementary decoration in many mediums including bronze sculpture, paintings and rugs, its early appearance, circa 2000 BCE on Bronze Age Central Asian seals, pre-dates the dawn of Buddhism.[40] Later regarded by Tibetan Buddhism as one of the eight auspicious symbols, it represents "destiny, fate and inevitability" inflected with a sense of longevity (Eiland, 30).

Fig. 2

---

39 for Anatolian pottery from 5500 BCE, see Mellaart, 117, Plate LXIX, Fig. 1; for Bronze Age Central Asian seals, see Masson, 151, Fig. 1, Altyn-Depe, seal from excavation 7, face side, and Hiebert, 379, Fig. 6(b), an unfinished red stearite seal

40 P'Yankova, L., 360, Fig. 4, #18

The crossed *vajra* motif or, as it is commonly called, the double *dorje*, is ubiquitous. Considered a source of strength and constancy, the *vajra*—an instrument essential to Tibetan Buddhist practice—is also a symbol of the "heart of knowledge as well as the emptiness of the sky".[41] Buddhist ceremonies often use a single *vajra* with a bulbous head at either end (Fig. 3); when depicted in weavings, the two *vajras* are placed perpendicular to one another and form a talismanic cross.

Fig. 3

Other Buddhist as well as Taoist and Confucian symbols may be found in Tibetan rugs. These include classical art motifs such as parasols, bats, flaming jewels, clouds, (Figs. 4, 5, 6, 7 respectively), cranes, fish, books, peony and chrysanthemum flowers, the lotus and the 'three fruits' comprising peach, pomegranate and citron.

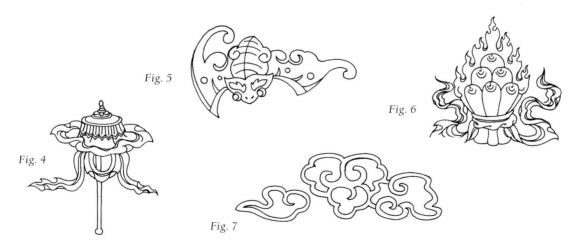

Fig. 5

Fig. 6

Fig. 4

Fig. 7

---

41 taken from keithdowman.net. Keith Dowman is a Buddhist scholar living in Kathmandu, Nepal, and the author of several books on the *dharma*.

Geometric Designs

PLATE 24

Patterns which repeat across an entire field comprise some of the more interesting types of rug designs. The field pattern in Plate 24, an integral component of the Tibetan design pool, replicates motifs which bear a resemblance to those found on an ancient felt

(shown right) excavated at Pazyryk in the Altai mountains and dated to approximately 300 BCE. As previously suggested, the apparent continuity of a design tradition may be attributed to a possible shared ancestry that links certain segments of the Tibetan people to Indo-Scythian tribes.

Another design type, a lattice containing motifs that resemble the 'erre' *gol* from the Yomud Turkmen design group, is rather startling, but may, once again, be attributed to shared ethnic origins. Theorists such as Terrence McKenna have speculated that memories of pattern might be inherited, passed on from weaver to weaver through a kind of 'collective unconscious' or even genetic code. Another possibile explanation for coincidences of motif, in addition to the more typical processes of direct and indirect diffusion, is 'independent invention,' where disparate peoples in diverse locales invent the same pattern without mutual influence or interaction.[42]

---

42 The term 'independent invention' is based upon private correspondence with Elizabeth Barber, July 2, 2004. My intepretation of direct diffusion would involve dispersal of patterns through migration of specific peoples while indirect diffusion might be the result of the appropriation of design through cultural exchange.

Medallions

In the realm of Tibetan rug design, the medallion or *gol* motif is one of the most popular and enduring. There are two types of medallions. The first is composed of stylized, floral roundels, some of which bear a likeness to Chinese silk textiles; and the second, found on many older rugs, clearly relates to the stepped polygon devices seen on carpets from the Central Asian steppe lands. This latter type is often found in a 3-medallion orientation, with the central medallion usually highlighted or drawn in a somewhat different manner. Hans Bidder argues that the 3-medallion design, when observed in rugs from East Turkestan, is derived from Buddhist iconography, implying that the central medallion designates the place where the Buddha, flanked by attendants on either side, is seated. This particular interpretation may be applied to Tibetan rugs. But these medallions, found on the older rugs of the plateau, have a distinctly archaic drawing quite similar to that employed by weavers located to the west, in Xinjiang and West Turkestan.

PLATES 38, 39, 40

PLATES 43, 45, 46

Although ubiquitous in Central Asian weavings, the inspiration for this medallion or *gol* ornament remains a mystery. While numerous rug scholars have linked Tibetan and Buddhist motifs, most have failed to realize that many of the designs we recognize as Buddhist are actually products of far older histories, beliefs and traditions; iconography and forms Buddhism simply appropriated for its own semiotic elaborations. The theory that these shapes are derived from the designs found on Yuan Dynasty Chinese porcelains may be correct but is somewhat misleading.[43] The Yuan dynasty marked a period of Mongol rather than Chinese rule in China, thus the patterns produced at this time may, in fact, reflect an older Central Asian aesthetic.[44]

Viken Sassouni has argued that certain types of *gols* on Caucasian rugs are derived from the floor plans of Armenian Christian churches. Yet, as he briefly notes, these early churches were often built on the very foundations of the pagan structures they replaced (HALI Vol. 4, #1). While Sassouni's theory has generally been accepted among scholars in the field, Christoph Huber has extended it, arguing for a more archaic inspiration by

---

43 *Turkmen—Tribal Carpets and Traditions*, edited by Louise Mackie and Jon Thompson, 61
44 *Chinese Rugs—Art from the Steppes*, Thomas Cole, HALI #67, 74–77

comparing the shapes of Anatolian and Central Asian *gol* forms to the seals and floor plans of the Late Bronze Age period (circa 2000 BCE) BMAC temple complexes excavated in Turkmenistan and northern Afghanistan.[45]

Asko Parpola, Professor of Indology at the University of Helsinki, has linked several of these BMAC architectural forms—including the concentric circles-within-a-square layout and T-shaped corridors—to mandalas (Fig. 8), specifically to those found on Tibetan *thangkas*. He also connects these mandala forms to Chinese Han Dynasty TLV mirror designs dating from approximately 200 BCE, commenting that "indeed the pattern is so distinctive there can hardly be doubt about the continuity of traditions" (Parpola, 265). As he illustrates how the BMAC temple floor plans influenced later Buddhist *stupas* and Tantric Yogini temples, as well as the even later Han Period mirrors, he also emphasizes that "the occurrence of the TLV pattern of ultimately BMAC origin on the round metal mirrors of China is not without significance. ...round metal mirrors with a handle or with a loop are known widely from Central and Inner Asia from the Late Bronze Age [1650–1050 BCE]; by the end of the second millennium BC the metal mirror had become part of the standard equipment of the mounted nomad" (Parpola, 265). Great numbers of metal mirrors have been excavated from the graves of mounted nomad warriors, both female and male, in various Bronze and Iron Age archeological sites throughout the Eurasian steppes. Moreover, as Parpola asserts, the Chinese adopted the use of the mirror from indigenous nomadic cultures situated in Xinjiang.

Fig. 8 Two examples of mandala patterns found on BMAC seals

---

45 *Old Motifs*, Christoph Huber, Ghereh, #22, 1999

The significance of the relationship between these mirrors and *stupas*, seals and building floor plans is primarily speculative, but Parpola relates these structures and motifs to sacred cosmograms, the means by which people visualize and engage their own numinous essence as well as that of the world. The T-shaped forms on the TLV mirrors may be linked to the gates of imperial tombs—the gates between worlds—while the four quadrants represent the four seas. It is not irrelevant to a consideration of Tibetan rug motifs that the spirit icons for these four directions are a tortoise/snake, a dragon, a bird and a tiger, and the center is represented by a star (Parpola, 265). Likewise, definitions of the mandala pattern link it to a gated palace or cosmic mountain resting on a lotus flower that rises out of a cosmic sea; contemplating this vulviform gateway symbolically recreates the journey to enlightenment (Shaw, 26). *Stupas*—which symbolize the 'World Mountain,' the 'Dome of Heaven' and the 'Hallowed 'Womb'—exhibit a strong connection to these other forms (Fiero, 211). As Singer notes, "were the *stupas* actually reconstructed, the arrangement would form a three dimensional mandala, the outer *stupas* oriented to the four cardinal points of the compass" (Singer, 11).

Stepping farther back in time, we do know that mirrors were indispensable accoutrements of the oracles and shamans of pre-Buddhist, pre-Islamic Central Asian cultures, particularly the Turks, Mongols and other nomadic peoples. As far back as the Scythians, and no doubt much earlier, shamans were considered essential not only for personal healing but also political advice.[46] Similar traditions persist to this day in Tibet, with oracles often pictured wearing large bronze mirrors attached to their chests,

---

46 "Religious Beliefs" in *Nomads of Eurasia*, Vladimir N. Basilov and Natalya L. Zhukovskaya, 169

vehicles for interacting with the powerful forces that govern their community's very existence. It seems plausible that the medallion shapes in pile weavings may be linked to these distinctive and archaic patterns scholars have traced in other mediums, constituting, perhaps, a portal of their own, another kind of language for the histories, beliefs and myths that weave past and future inextricably into an ongoing texture of presence.

Conclusion

The art of Tibetan rugs reflects a long weaving tradition, one that was probably imported at a very early date from the western fringes of the ancient Tibetan Empire and beyond, including Persia and parts of Central Asia. Originally a folk art practiced by the tribal and rural inhabitants of the plateau, it developed and grew as Tibet's sphere of power and affluence approached its zenith in the late 19th and early 20th centuries. Although the Tibetan aesthetic is often equated with that of the Far East and China, we would do well to keep in mind that the development of weaving in those regions was a later phenomenon, initiated by many of the same tribal peoples whose artistic sensibilities, from very early times, have left their mark on the Tibetan tradition. Not enough is known about the particular traditions or design pool of any specific region or people in mid-19th-century Tibet as documentary evidence is, for the most part, absent. What we do have is the rugs themselves. Those fortunate enough to have survived, carefully preserved for posterity in the homes of the people or in the storerooms of the monastic communities, provide a tangible view into the artistic legacy of a vanished era.

1

A typically Tibetan rendition, utilizing the penchant for depicting clouds. While not drawn in the curvilinear style related to weavings in a finer medium (i.e. silk), there is a distinctly 'tribal' effect achieved; the center of each cloud in the field resembles a tribal *tamghan* (tribal brand) or totemic ram's horn configuration. The simple attempt at placing a border on this rug suggests a pattern extending into infinity, another characteristic of Central Asian weaving.

Warp	: Z 2 S ivory wool
Weft	: 2 sheds ivory wool
Knots	: 3 + 4 ply yarn, wool
7h x 4v	= 28kpsi
Colors (8)	: lt. yellow / red / pink / blue-green / purple (faded) / med. blue / lt. blue / orange
Size	: 87cm x 175cm (34.2in x 68.8in)

2

An exercise in color and simplicity. Clearly intended for monastic use, the rich orange/gold color is unusual to be used in such abundance. The four swastikas in the corners compose the only real designs; the alternately opposed swastikas are drawn with no relevance to either the Bon-po or Buddhist version of this motif. Given the clear abrash, it is likely the field color is derived from a natural dyestuff, possibly tumeric.

Warp	: ivory + lt. orange wool plied cotton
Weft	: 1 shed lt. orange wool
Knots	: 3 + 4 ply yarn, wool
9h x 5v	= 45kpsi
Colors (2)	: orange / mustard gold
Size	: 89cm x 172cm (35in x 67.7in)

3

The coin-like medallions with a phoenix and snow lion contained within is a very unusual ornament, possibly one that is unique in my experience. The drawing of the phoenix is inspired by Chinese textiles from the Ming period; the squared-off wings are characteristic of those weavings. The whimsical, almost child-like drawing of the snow lion depicted in a frontal pose, is typically Tibetan. Lotus flowers alternate with birds and butterflies as the additional ornaments of these elaborate coin medallions.

Warp	: Z 2 S ivory wool
Weft	: 1 shed ivory wool
Knots	: 3 ply yarn, wool
9h x 5v	= 45kpsi
Colors (6)	: med. blue / lt. blue / orange / pink / tan / rose
Size	: 89cm x 164cm (35in x 64.5in)

4

A classic pattern inspired by Ming period Chinese textiles. The treatment of the design is typically Tibetan, with opposing pairs of dragons and phoenix playfully arranged in the field and a large lotus in the center. But the drawing of the wings of the birds is interpreted in the style of Ming period textiles as is the animated expression on the faces of the dragons, characterized by the bulging eyes, protruding tongue and serpentine body. Published analogy, Woven Jewels, Plate 45

Warp	: Z 2 S ivory wool
Weft	: 1 shed ivory wool + brown wool (alternating)
Knots	: 3 ply yarn, wool
12h x 4.5v	= 54kpsi
Colors (14)	: red / lt. red / pink / dk. blue / med. blue / yellow / blue-green / lt. green / lt. coral / orange / beige / ivory / lt. pink / khaki green
Size	: 86cm x 173cm (33.8in x 68.1in)

5

Four sinuous dragon bodies compose the principal design of this particular rug. When viewed at a distance, considering the four bodies at one time, they form the outline of the Chinese character *shou*, which symbolizes long life. The spotted heads of these dragons mimic a Ming period aesthetic, but apparently the weaver was having problems keeping the proportions correct as the heads tend to be flattened, a product of ratio of knots on the horizontal and vertical axis. The border—with a modified, simple 'T' pattern—speaks of a different aesthetic, as does the very simple minor border framing the field. The original red dyed felted cloth remains intact, stabilizing both the edges and ends.

Warp	: 5 ply ivory wool
Weft	: 2 sheds ivory wool
Knots	: 3 + 4 ply yarn, wool
9h x 8v	= 72kpsi
Colors (11)	: red / lt. pink / yellow / dk. blue / lt. blue / blue-green / tan / brownish maroon / ivory / coral red / lt. orange
Size	: 85cm x 175cm (33.4in x 68.9in)

6

Playful, sinuously drawn dragons with expressive faces are reminiscent of Qing period textiles. This rug was undoubtedly made for monastic use as is suggested by the yellow field. The stiffer version of the cloud/mountain border as well as the drawing of the clouds situated in the four corners of the field are highly suggestive of a rigid workshop atmosphere where the pattern was undoubtedly executed from a graph. Published analogy, Kuløy, Plate 65

Warp	: 5 ply cotton
Weft	: 2 sheds ivory wool + some dk. brown wool
Knots	: 3 + 4 ply yarn, wool
9h x 7v	= 63kpsi
Colors (12)	: dk. blue / med. blue / tan / brown / red / blue-green / lt. blue-green / gray brown / walnut brown / rose / orange / ivory
Size	: 85cm x 163cm (33.5in x 64.1in)

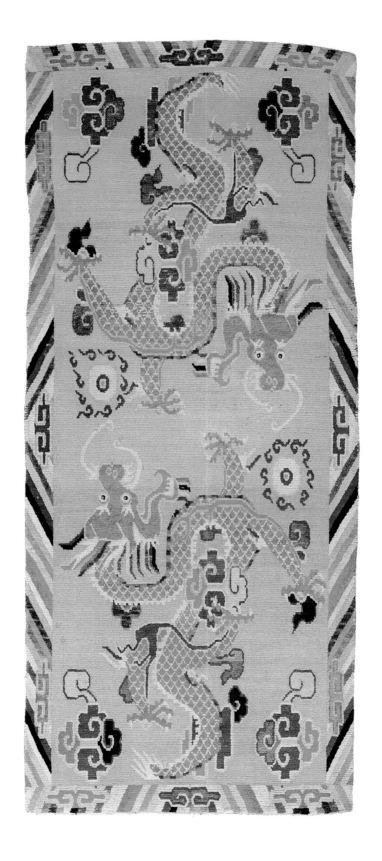

7

An interesting type of rug, typical of a particular late 19th- or early 20th-century production, with a minimal palette. Two shades of blue and ivory wool are used to execute a pattern more often associated with the stencil patterned felts thought to come from Mongolia, which are also executed with a minimalist palette. A playful bird flies among flowers springing forth from water, surrounded by a very intricately drawn minor border that is framed by a beautifully drawn primary border containing many Buddhist icons.

Warp	: 1 S ivory wool
Weft	: 1 shed lt. brown wool
Knots	: 3 ply yarn, wool
8h x 5v	= 40kpsi
Colors (3)	: dk. blue / med. blue / lt. blue beige
Size	: 91cm x 166cm (35.8in x 65.4in)

8

A classic weaving exhibiting many Buddhist symbols, all elegantly arranged on an unusual ivory field (natural sheep's wool). The birds are drawn in a classic manner, with one foot lifted and a flower grasped in the beak—an image seen in silk weavings dating as far back as 1000 years. The plethora of Buddhist imagery suggests this rug was made on special order in one of the many workshops that existed at the end of the 19th or early 20th century.

Warp	: 4 ply cotton
Weft	: 1 shed ivory wool
Knots	: 3 + 4 ply yarn, wool
11h x 7v	= 77kpsi
Colors (11)	: tan / red / rust / dk. blue / lt. blue / blue-green / lt. pink / lemon yellow / sienna / mustard yellow / terracotta
Size	: 90cm x 182cm (35.4in x 71.6in)

9

The actual weaving process of this rug must have been very difficult. To construct the fretwork pattern as the ground of the rug with large, boldly drawn lotus designs is unusual, evidence of the artistry of the weaver and mastery over the physical materials—the loom and the different colored woolen yarns. Drawn with a slight asymmetry, the flowers float effortlessly over the tightly controlled grid below.

Warp	: 1 S ivory wool
Weft	: 1 shed ivory wool + dk. brown wool
Knots	: 3 + 4 ply yarn, wool
7h x 4v	= 28kpsi
Colors (11)	: dk. blue / med. blue / lt. blue / ivory / maroon / red / blue-green / orange-red / lt. pink / apricot / tan
Size	: 81cm x 143cm (31.9in x 56.3in)

■ 67

10

An interesting and decorative composition, with three 'crane' medallions dominating a field surrounded by a classic cloud/mountain border, all derived from a later Chinese textile prototype. Cranes are associated with symbols of long life and are often found in the Tibetan rug design pool.

Warp	: 4 ply cotton
Weft	: 1 shed gray brown wool
Knots	: 3 + 4 ply yarn, wool
12h x 8v	= 96kpsi
Colors (11)	: tan / red / dk. blue / lt. blue / yellow / green / rust-orange / blue-green / pink / ivory / sienna
Size	: 90cm x 181cm (35.4in x 71.2in)

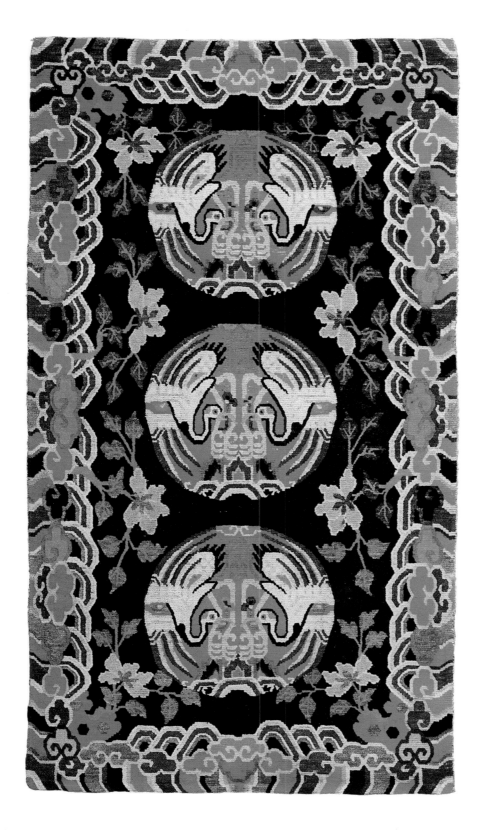

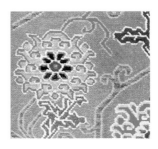

11

A classic design depicting flowers and twisting vines with leaves. The balanced composition is pleasing as is the ground color which serves as an attractive contrast for the colorful flowers. The simple border, a version of the Tibetan 'wave' motif, is seen in various forms throughout the Turkic weaving world. Possibly intended for monastic use due to the gold ground color, it is either the top piece of a saddle rug or a mat on which to sit.

Warp	: Z 2 S ivory wool
Weft	: 1 shed ivory wool
Knots	: 3 ply yarn, wool
7h x 6v	= 42kpsi
Colors (10)	: gold-brown / dk. blue / med. blue / lt. blue / coral red / lt. pink / blue-green / lt. blue-green / mustard yellow / maroon
Size	: 58cm x 86cm (22.8in x 33.8in)

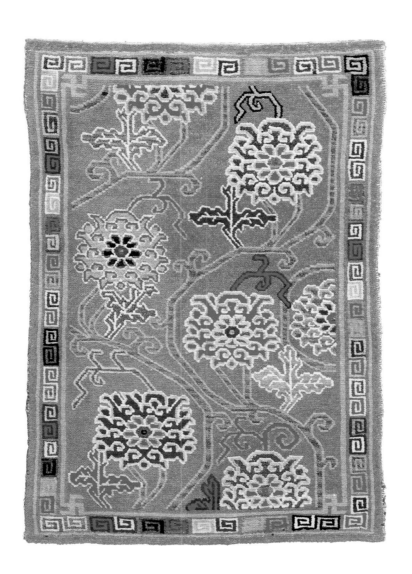

12

An interesting composition with the unusual depiction of a seeded fruit, possibly pomegranate, a traditional fertility symbol used throughout Central Asia. This rug is interesting for another reason—the use of two colors of dyed woolen yarn plied together and employed within a single knot to produce a mottled effect. This technique is one that is associated more with the later workshop productions rather than earlier village weavings.

Warp	: Z 2 S ivory wool + brown with white plied
Weft	: 1 shed ivory wool
Knots	: 3 ply yarn, wool
8h x 5v	= 40kpsi
Colors (13)	: walnut brown / med. blue / lt. blue / red / pink / dk. brown maroon / blue-green / lt. orange / pink (faded) / yellow / pink / salmon (faded) / lt. green
Size	: 92cm x 169cm (36.2in x 66.5in)

13

An interesting pattern which is somehow reminiscent of textile design, not necessarily Chinese but Central Asian brocade. The dark gold lines that tie the design together is very reminiscent of a type I have seen elsewhere in European-inspired brocades made for an eastern market. With the elaborately articulated lotus flowers, the Tibetan interpretation of the design is unmistakable.

Warp	: 4 ply cotton, machine spun
Weft	: 1 shed ivory wool
Knots	: 3 + 4 ply yarn, wool
10h x 7v	= 70kpsi
Colors (10)	: red / orange / blue-green / lt. blue / dk. blue / brownish maroon / lavender / brownish orange / gray brown / yellow green
Size	: 88cm x 170cm (34.6in x 66.9in)

14

A somewhat eccentric composition with drawing reminiscent of an earlier aesthetic. The curled patterns extending out from what appear to be flowers are akin to the ancient ram's horn symbol seen throughout Central Asia; this is especially pronounced at the top and bottom of the field. The bold drawing executed in an abnormally light, almost pastel palette is quite unusual and one that hardly adheres to the standard perception of a reliance upon primary colors. The scrolling vine and tendril border with blossoms regularly sprinkled throughout is an unusual design, one that is seldom used in this way to frame the field of a carpet. Published analogy, Kuløy, Plate 38; Myers, Plate 47

Warp	: Z 2 S ivory + a bit of brown wool
Weft	: 2 sheds brown wool
Knots	: 3 + 4 ply yarn, wool
8h x 4v	= 32kpsi
Colors (13)	: tan / maroon / lilac / lt. coral red / med. green abrash / yellow / med. blue / lt. blue / coral red / charcoal blue / ivory / lt. orange / pink
Size	: 94cm x 169cm (37in x 66.5in)

15

A typical design composition consisting of floral forms emerging out of a classic wave/mountain/cloud base, patterned after Qing period Chinese silk brocade. Such details as the finely articulated curvilinear leaves and the white drops of water on the blue background suggest the weaver was possibly looking at a textile during the weaving process. The colorful palette typifies the Tibetan penchant to liven up the typically drab surroundings in which they lived.

Warp	: 6 ply cotton
Weft	: 2 sheds brown wool
Knots	: 3 + 4 ply yarn, wool
11h x 5.5v	= 60.5kpsi
Colors (9)	: dk. blue / med. blue / lt. blue / orange / salmon / lt. pink / rust / ivory / lt. yellow (faded)
Size	: 89cm x 158cm (35in x 62.2in)

16

A fabulous drawing of a traditional design with elaborately articulated leaves, complete with veins and irregular yet well-defined and realistic edges. This drawing is directly inspired by Yuan period textiles and it is likely the weavers had access to those old weavings. The varied palette with a wealth of color and the delicate drawing of the tendrils, leaves and flowers make this a very special type.

Warp	: Z 2 S ivory wool
Weft	: 1 shed ivory wool
Knots	: 4 ply yarn, wool
8h x 5v	= 40kpsi
Colors (12)	: walnut brown abrash / dk. blue / med. blue / lt. blue / green / red / maroon / mustard yellow / lavender / brownish maroon / lt. pink / lt. olive green
Size	: 91cm x 168cm (35.8in x 66.1in)

17

A beautifully colored example of the lotus/vine motif. The abrashed blue ground is exceptionally well-handled, and it is interesting that the weaver chose to use a similar color to shade some of the flowers. This unusual juxtaposition of similar colors is featured in older weavings from Central Asia. The articulation of the tendrils and the veins of the leaves indicate the level of artistry practiced by the weaver who was obviously very familiar with this pattern.

Warp	: Z 2 S ivory wool
Weft	: 2 sheds ivory wool
Knots	: 4 ply yarn, wool
8h x 6v	= 48kpsi
Colors (10)	: dk. blue-green / lt. blue-green / dk. blue / med. blue / red / pink / dk. aubergine / lt. tan / ivory / caramel brown
Size	: 85cm x 164cm (33.5in x 64.5in)

18

Large lotus flowers springing forth from water and cloud patterns at either end recall the aesthetic of Chinese silk brocade weaving. The chrysanthemums flowering from a tree bearing a seeded fruit (a symbol of fertility) are attractively drawn and provide a balance to the design. The articulation of the leaves, with carefully drawn 'veins' on the surface, is a relatively uncommon feature, denoting a certain quality and the care with which this rug was made. Published analogy, Myers, Plate 39

Warp	: Z 2 S blue + ivory wool
Weft	: 1 shed gray brown wool
Knots	: 3 + 4 ply yarn, wool
9h x 5v	= 45kpsi
Colors (14)	: dk. blue / med. blue / lt. blue / ivory / red / green / lt. green / pink / blue-green / mustard yellow / rust orange / lt. gray tan / mauve / lt. pink
Size	: 94cm x 183cm (37in x 72in)

19

A warp faced back rug from Tibet with the traditional 3-medallion design format. This is a strange technique but one that gives warmth because of its very thick pile. The pattern seen here is not part of the early design pool of rugs woven in this technique. Curiously, the vestigial borders at the top and bottom of the field suggest a version of the wave or meandering 'T' border, an unusual feature to be seen so randomly placed within the field.

Warp	: Z 2 S ivory wool
Weft	: 2 sheds ivory wool
Knots	: 3 ply cabled yarn, wool
3h x 2v	= 6kpsi
Colors (5)	: med. blue / lt. blue / lt. coral / brownish maroon / khaki green (faded)
Size	: 81cm x 155cm (31.8in x 61in)

20

An older design for rugs of this warp faced back type but somewhat unusual for a rug woven in the *khaden* size. The concentric squares of color are a feature of older examples woven in this archaic technique. The pile on such weavings is usually a cabled yarn rather than combed and refined yarn. The use of cabled yarn is also seen in other Central Asian weavings intended for cold weather climates.

Warp	: Z 2 S ivory wool (a few of brown + ivory shed)
Weft	: 1 shed brown + ivory wool
Knots	: 3 ply yarn, wool
3h x 2v	= 6kpsi
Colors (3)	: lt. red / blue-green (faded) / med. blue (faded)
Size	: 76cm x 163cm (29.9in x 64.1in) — excludes fringe

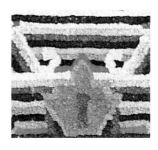

21

A pair of pillow cushions, an unusual format of weaving in Tibet. Such pillows were usually commissioned by wealthy patrons rather than made for traditional domestic use. The field design consists of a stylized mountain/wave pattern in a very linear rendition. Interestingly, the red cloth sewn onto the sides consists of woven silk brocade rather than the plain red cloth that is usually used.

Warp	: Z ivory twist wool
Weft	: 1 shed ivory wool
Knots	: 4 + 5 ply yarn, wool
7h x 5v	= 35kpsi
Colors (7)	: lt. blue / med. blue / dk. blue / green / yellow / red / brown
Size	: 60.5cm x 38.5cm (23.8in x 15.1in)

22

An elegantly drawn mat or top piece of a saddle set. The beautifully articulated lotus with tendrils are bold, contributing to a harmoniously balanced image. The bats seen in the field composition blend into the foliate pattern, with little contrast given to their bodies through outlining and the use of similar colors to the tendrils. A remarkably sophisticated and artistic weaving of which I cannot say I recall seeing many similarly drawn examples.

Warp	: 4 ply cotton
Weft	: 1 shed ivory wool
Knots	: 3 ply yarn, wool
12h x 7v	= 84kpsi
Colors (9)	: lemon yellow / red / pink / orange / blue-green / lt. orange / dk. blue / gray brown natural / walnut brown
Size	: 58cm x 72cm (22.8in x 28.3in)

23

An unusually ornate top piece of a saddle set. With a number of floral forms placed over the tight fretwork ground pattern, such a design calls upon the weaver to have complete command of the pattern and the loom. Elegantly composed and flawlessly executed, this is a very unusual example of weaving from the early 20th century.

Warp	: 6 ply cotton
Weft	: 1 shed ivory wool
Knots	: 4 ply yarn, wool
12h x 6v	= 72kpsi
Colors (6)	: dk. blue / med. blue / lt. yellow / red / pink / dk. salmon / purple brown (faded)
Size	: 60cm x 74cm (23.6in x 29.1in)

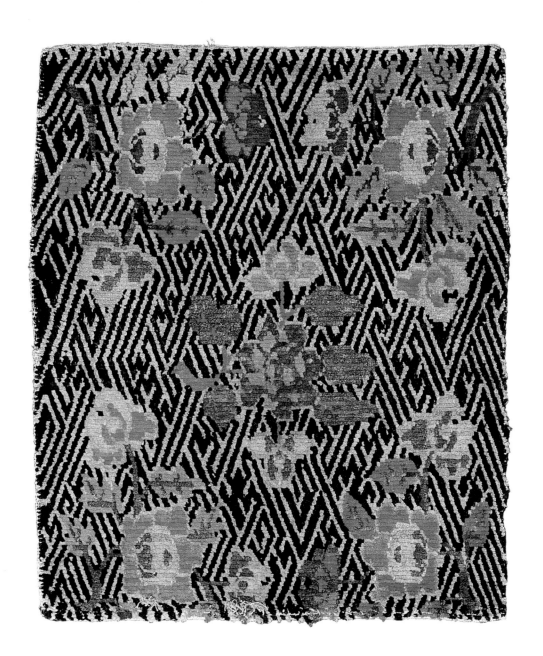

24

An interesting pattern that is used occasionally. Often called a 'fish scale' design, it may very well trace its origins to an ancient felt excavated at Pazyryk by Rudenko and presently housed in the Hermitage Museum in St. Petersburg. Seen here with a beautiful palette characterized by a very nice aubergine color, the rug can be safely dated to the early 20th century. The blossoms scattered in the Greek key or meandering 'T' border suggests this conjecture. Published analogy, Kuløy, Plate 86

Warp	: Z 2 S wool
Weft	: 2 sheds ivory wool
Knots	: 5 ply yarn, wool
8h x 4v	= 32kpsi
Colors (7)	: red / lt. red / dk. blue / med. blue / lt. blue / lt. violet / brown
Size	: 67cm x 180cm (26.3in x 70.8in)

25

Another complex field composition consisting of the swastika fretwork pattern that was popularized, perhaps, in Chinese wood furniture from where it found its way into the medium of weaving. Again, we see a border with a wealth of Buddhist iconography though the palette does not indicate monastic use. It was probably commissioned by a wealthy family in one of the sponsored weaving projects around either Shigatse or Gyantse. The use of indigo is exceptionally pleasing.

Warp	: Z 2 S 2 ivory wool
Weft	: 1 shed gray brown + ivory wool
Knots	: 4 ply yarn, wool
9h x 4.5v	= 40.5kpsi
Colors (2)	: dk. blue / lt. blue
Size	: 87cm x 161cm (34.2in x 63.3in)

26

A lovely rug exhibiting an overall lattice pattern, a form of design that is ubiquitous throughout all the Central Asian weaving cultures. The beautifully dyed blue ground provides a lovely contrast to the unusual treatment of the lattice itself, delineated in various alternating colors. This treatment contributes to rather lively and dynamic visuals that are not apparent in other analogous examples. The ornament within the lattice recalls the Turkmen 'erre' *gol*.

Warp	: Z 2 S ivory wool
Weft	: 1 shed ivory wool + dk. brown wool
Knots	: 3 + 4 ply yarn, wool
7h x 4v	= 28kpsi
Colors (11)	: dk. blue / med. blue / lt. blue / ivory / maroon / red / blue-green / orange red / lt. pink / apricot / tan
Size	: 81cm x 143cm (31.8in x 56.2in)

27

An interesting version of a lattice patterned rug with an unusual palette used in the field. The primary motif seen is the Tibetan version of the so-called 'erre' *gol*, an ornament seen in the weavings of the Yomud. The minor 'pearl' border frames the field, which in turn is placed adjacent to another minor border filled with what is often referred to as the 'rice grain' pattern. The Greek key or meandering 'T' border is given a three-dimensional aspect, a version of this classic drawing that dates the piece to circa 1900 or perhaps a bit later. Published analogy, Kuløy, Plate 88

Warp	: Z 2 S ivory wool
Weft	: 2 sheds ivory wool
Knots	: 3 ply yarn, wool
8h x 5v	= 40kpsi
Colors (8)	: dk. blue / lt. blue / coral red / blue-green / yellow / lt. pink / red / lt. blue-green
Size	: 73cm x 129cm (28.7in x 50.7in)

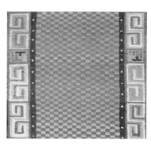

28

An interesting checkerboard rug, unusual for the fact that it has such a developed, bold and graphic border. Apparently intended for monastic use due to the predominantly orange field color, the border—composed of large scale 'S' motifs—is probably a vestigial memory of an ancient aesthetic. Such 'S' borders are known in Central Asian weavings of antiquity including Turkmen weavings (where they are usually used as a minor border) and Anatolian village rugs.

Warp	: 6 ply cotton
Weft	: 1 shed ivory + brown wool
Knots	: 4 ply yarn, wool
6h x 4v	= 24kpsi
Colors (10)	: orange / red / lt. red (faded) / pink (faded) / lt. blue / blue-green / burnt orange / dk. burgundy / natural brown overdyed / blue
Size	: 73cm x 140cm (28.7in x 55.1in)

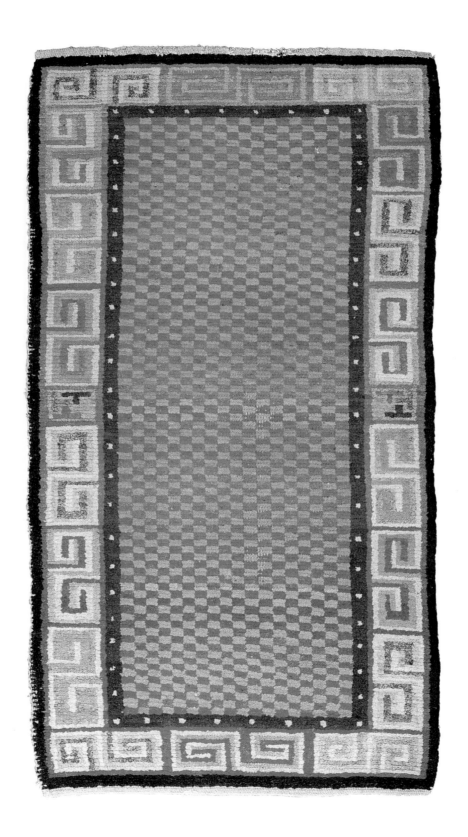

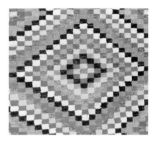

29

An extremely unusual variation of the checkerboard theme forming concentric diamonds defined by color changes. The overall composition could very well be identified as Uzbek if not for the distinctive cut loop method of knotting. The very nature of the pattern is prone to a certain stiffness, which is avoided here probably because of uneven warps and wefts; this uneveness could possibly be the result of the spin of the wool or the manner in which the loom was strung to begin with.

Warp	: Z 2 S gray wool
Weft	: 2 sheds black wool, 5 ply
Knots	: 3 ply yarn, wool
6h x 5v	= 30kpsi
Colors (11)	: red / maroon / orange / yellow / khaki green / dk. blue / dk. blue-black / fuschia / ivory / charcoal blue / turquoise
Size	: 79cm x 157cm (31.1in x 61.8in)

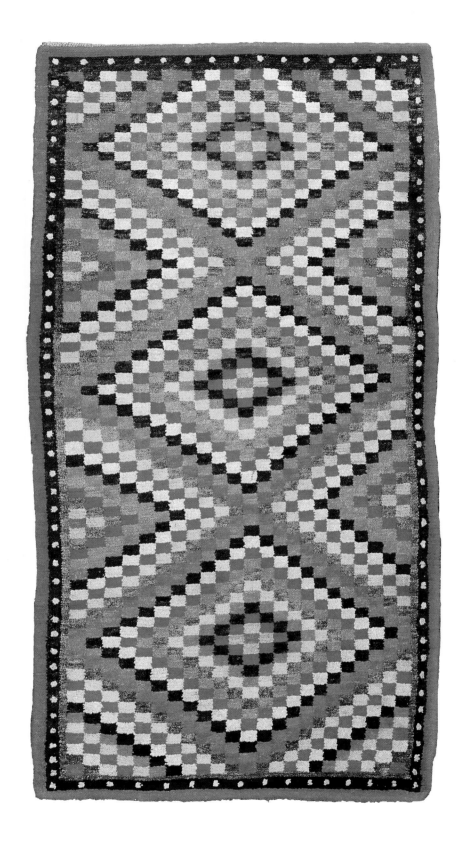

30

An interesting version of the checkerboard design type, except this time with clearly drawn crosses within alternating squares. Emphasizing the talismanic nature of the pattern, the weavers chose to clearly delineate crosses in all the squares with alternating colors. Given a green border surrounding the entire composition, one realizes this is a true carpet made with a purpose, as most checkerboard rugs do not have solid colored woven edges.

Warp	: Z 2 S ivory wool
Weft	: 2 sheds ivory wool
Knots	: 3, 4 + 5 ply yarn, wool
7h x 4v	= 28kpsi
Colors (7)	: lt. green / green / brown / yellow / red / violet (faded) / med. blue
Size	: 86cm x 173cm (33.8in x 68.1in)

31

An eye-dazzling checkerboard design rug. With larger scale drawing, rugs of this type become infinitely more pleasing than those with small checks. The abrash and color changes melt into each other, resulting in a very fluid composition. Rugs of this type exhibit such mastery of dyeing and blending of colors, they seem to refute the idea that checkerboard rugs were woven by students learning the craft.

Warp	: Z 2 S ivory + lt. brown wool
Weft	: 1 shed ivory + lt. brown wool
Knots	: 4 ply yarn, wool
8.5h x 6v	= 51kpsi
Colors (5)	: blue-green / lt. red / red / lt. violet / raspberry (faded)
Size	: 93cm x 180cm (36.6in x 70.8in)

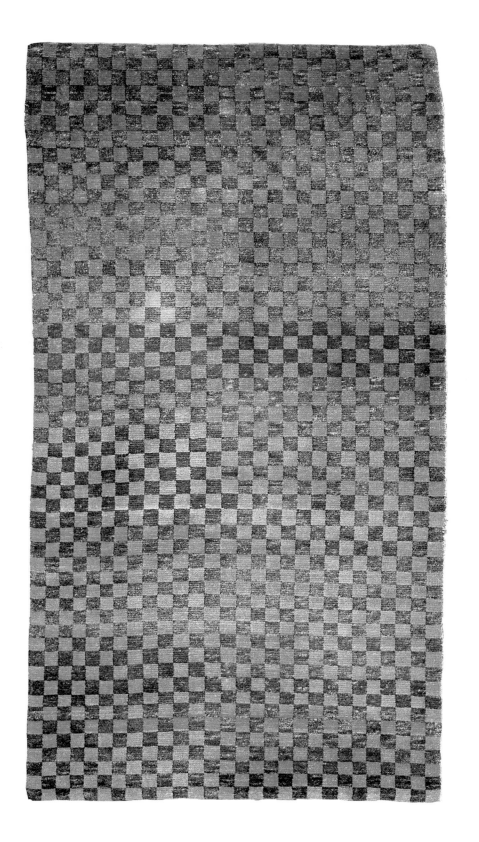

■ 111

32

If there was ever any question about what the checkerboard motifs represent, this cross/check rug dispels that confusion, indicating the truly talismanic nature of the pattern. With clear crosses drawn in five squares of color, alternating with the stepped polygon pattern (another larger, more elaborate cross), the palette seen here is quite pleasing. A combination of woolen yarns alternately colored in dye baths of varying strengths, the abrash is quite attractive and the rug has a definite presence.

Warp	: Z 2 S ivory wool
Weft	: 1 shed brown wool
Knots	: 3 ply yarn, wool
7h x 5v	= 35kpsi
Colors (2)	: dk. blue / lt. blue
Size	: 75cm x 163cm (29.5in x 64.1in)

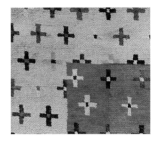

33

An interesting rug with the so-called 'tigma' pattern mimicking the woolen tie-dyed textiles of similar patterning and color. Such textiles are fashioned into long runners, cutting dyed woolen cloth and sewing it with cushioning inside. This rug was woven to emulate these dyed woolen textiles. Published analogy, Kuløy, Plate 92; Cole, Hali #49, 18, Plate 3

Warp	: Z 2 S ivory wool
Weft	: 2 sheds ivory wool
Knots	: 4 + 5 ply yarn, wool
6h x 3v	= 18kpsi
Colors (7)	: red / lt. red / dk. blue / blue-green / lt. yellow / lt. orange / ivory
Size	: 80cm x 157.5cm (31.5in x 62in)

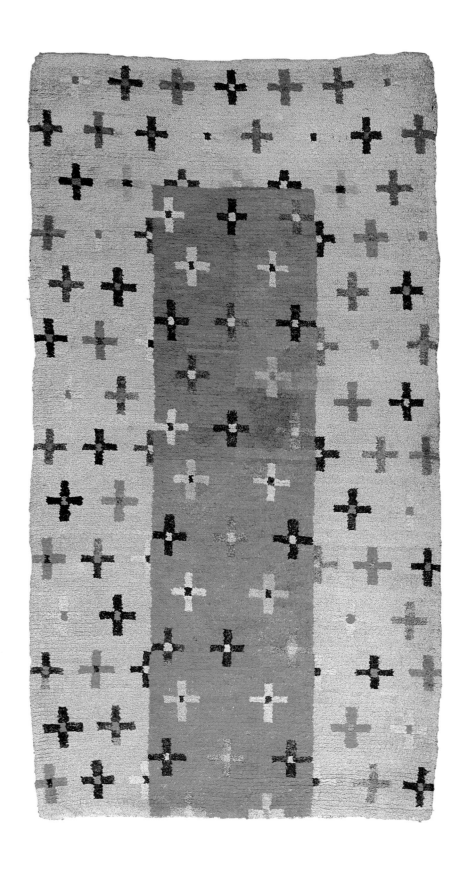

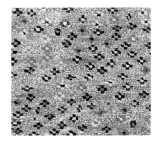

34

A tour-de-force of spontaneity. Rarely does the Tibetan aesthetic allow for such a novel and utterly random use of patterning. Seemingly devoid of the codified aesthetic one sees in the weavings from other Central Asian cultures, still the Tibetan design pool allows for only so much innovation. This rug breaks all established patterns and is unique in my experience. The simple crosses arbitrarily covering the field represent talismans to ensure good luck and ward off the evil eye.

Warp	: Z 2 S ivory wool
Weft	: 2 sheds ivory wool
Knots	: 4 ply yarn, wool
8h x 5v	= 40kpsi
Colors (8)	: red / salmon / dk. blue / lt. watery blue / ivory / khaki tan / rose (faded) / blue-green
Size	: 70.5cm x 150.5cm (27.7in x 59.2in)

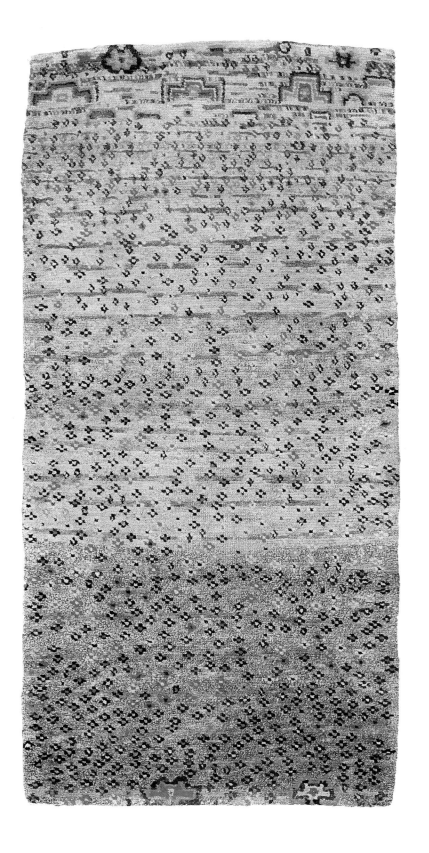

35

An interesting composition, rather abstract and executed with a balance and sensitivity not immediately apparent. The combination of elements, consisting of small rosette flower heads with another abstract form devoid of curvilinear lines but intended to represent another flower, is interesting. All these are situated on a blue field and surrounded by a woven pile dyed in red to mimic the cloth that is often attached to Tibetan rugs to secure the edges and ends.

Warp	: Z 2 S ivory wool
Weft	: 1 shed ivory + brown + red wool
Knots	: 2 + 3 ply yarn, wool
9h x 5v	= 45kpsi
Colors (8)	: dk. blue abrash / coral red / blue-green / beige / yellow / lt. pink / chartreuse / ivory
Size	: 78cm x 141cm (30.7in x 55.5in)

36

A beautifully dyed rug with a lovely ground color. The abrash is extremely attractive here, with varying shades of green, blue/green and yellow/green. The blossoms arranged in a seemingly orderly fashion on the surface are given no particular arrangement as defined by color. Like lilies floating on a lake, the weavers achieved an extremely pleasing aesthetic and, undoubtedly, the rug was considered special at the time it was woven.

Warp	: Z 2 S lt. brown wool
Weft	: 1 shed gray brown wool
Knots	: 3, 4 + 5 ply yarn, wool
7h x 7v	= 49kpsi
Colors (7)	: blue-green / dk. blue / lt. blue / orange / purple / tan / pink
Size	: 82cm x 145cm (32.2in x 57in)

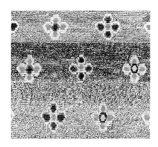

37

This rug provides a prime example of the technique of plying different colored strands of wool together to achieve a distinctive color change. The field consists of blue yarns plied with ivory wool, creating a watery, speckled effect. The geometricized flowers appear to float, imparting a three-dimensional aspect to the surface.

Warp	: Z 2 S ivory wool
Weft	: 2 sheds Z spun ivory wool
Knots	: 3 + 4 ply yarn, wool
8h x 5v	= 40kpsi
Colors (6)	: dk. blue / med. blue / lt. blue / orange / lt. pink (faded) / orange red
Size	: 84cm x 164cm (33in x 64.5in)

38

The intense yellow color used here suggests the possibility that this rug was intended for the use of a high lama. The fine materials and unusual color as well as the grand scale in which the brocade pattern is depicted seem appropriate for use by such an esteemed personage. The fine drawing of the pattern with details not usually encountered is evidence of the care with which this rug was woven.

Warp	: 9 ply cotton
Weft	: 2 sheds lt. yellow wool
Knots	: 4 ply yarn, wool
8h x 5v	= 40kpsi
Colors (2)	: golden yellow / ivory
Size	: 86cm x 162cm (33.8in x 63.7in)

39

Another weaving exhibiting the classic roundel patterns derived from Chinese silk brocades. It is not common to see borders used on rugs of this design type. An archaic motif is employed, in this instance, a 'wave' pattern from which the Greek key or meandering 'T' border is ultimately derived. The traditional use of a cloth to bind the ends and edges is still intact. Tibetan selvedges are unstable, and the manner in which the edges and ends are finished encourages unraveling. The use of color seen here is extraordinary. Published analogy, Kuløy, Plate 97

Warp	: 5 ply cotton
Weft	: 1 shed lt. gray wool
Knots	: 3 + 4 ply yarn, wool
10h x 6v	= 60kpsi
Colors (2)	: green with abrash / dk. blue-green
Size	: 74cm x 150cm (29.1in x 59in)

40

The brocade pattern, derived from Chinese silk textiles, is drawn on a larger scale with the use of reciprocal space, where the ground pattern within the medallions seen in light blue 'reads' more true, is more immediately apparent to the eye than the primary pattern seen in darker blue. With the *shou* pattern in the middle of every roundel, the drawing is very different from what one usually sees in other rugs of this design type.

Warp	: Z 2 S ivory wool
Weft	: 1 shed ivory wool
Knots	: 4 ply yarn, wool
7h x 4v	= 28kpsi
Colors (4)	: dk. blue / blue-green / natural brown wool / blue overdye
Size	: 81cm x 182cm (31.8in x 71.6in)

41

A beautifully colored brocade medallion rug. The green dyes are exceptional with an attractive use of abrash. The design is enhanced by the presence of colorful 'ribbon' motifs. Finely articulated with lovely curvilinear lines of design, this rug may be dated to the late 19th century. The simple and bold Greek key border, the fine drawing and unusual color suggest an earlier dating than most rugs of this design type.

Warp	: Z 2 S brown + ivory wool
Weft	: 1 shed brown wool
Knots	: 5 ply yarn, wool
7h x 4v	= 28kpsi
Colors (8)	: chartreuse / yellow / red / pink / ivory / matted blue / blue-green / walnut brown
Size	: 84cm x 140cm (33in x 55.1in)

42

An extremely beautiful example of Tibetan weaving exhibiting a quality of color rarely seen. The beautifully abrashed green/blue-green ground color is wonderful, imparting a three-dimensionality to the design and giving the illusion of the round medallions floating over the surface of the weaving. Whether intended or not, the color changes are extremely artistic. It is also unusual to see medallions being repeated over the surface of a rug, rather than arranged in the typical 3-medallion format.

Warp	: gray S ply wool
Weft	: 1 shed gray wool
Knots	: 4 + 5 ply yarn, wool
7h x 4v	= 28kpsi
Colors (7)	: blue-green / dk. blue / lt. blue / red / yellow / brown / ivory
Size	: 89cm x 166cm (35in x 65.3in)

43

An archaic design of sublime beauty. The light blue ground color on which the red medallions rest provides an incredible contrast, imparting the illusion of a three-dimensional perspective. The 'transparent' medallions—with the same ground color seen in the body of the *gol*—is a rare feature, a treatment of design seldom encountered. The archaic medallions along with the very simple treatment of the meandering 'T' border with no minor borders and simple fretwork patterning in the corners suggest an older weaving, possibly as early as the mid-19th century.

Warp	: Z 2 S ivory wool
Weft	: 2 sheds ivory wool
Knots	: 4 + 5 ply yarn, wool
6h x 4v	= 24kpsi
Colors (6)	: red / lt. green / lt. blue abrash / dk. blue / natural brown / blue overdye
Size	: 56cm x 240cm (22in x 94.4in)

44

A lovely old example of weaving from the high plateau, a small runner of exceptional beauty and saturated colors. The Greek key or meandering 'T' border is handled in an archaic manner with none of the embellished three-dimensional coloring that marks later versions. The medallions are bold 'erre' *gol* variants with the classic 'four arrow' layout. The so-called 'frogs foot' pattern profusively covering the indigo blue field is quite nice, a classic Tibetan treatment of a very typical minor design element. In Central Asia, such motifs are often interpreted as trees and are representative of fertility.

Warp	: Z 2 S ivory wool
Weft	: 2 sheds ivory + brown + gray wool
Knots	: 3, 4 + 5 ply yarn, wool
6h x 4v	= 24kpsi
Colors (9)	: dk. blue / med. blue / lt. blue / coral red / lt. coral red / ivory / lt. blue-green / brown with blue overdye / natural brown
Size	: 60cm x 250cm (23.6in x 98.4in)

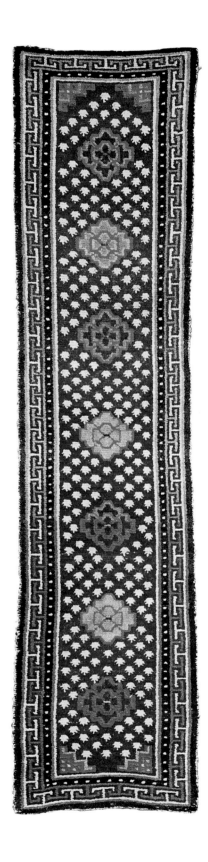

45

A lovely medallion with an incredibly green ground outlined in red and light blue situated in the center of a saturated indigo blue field. The clouds seen thoughout the field are an unusual design feature. Probably dating to the latter part of the 19th century, the relatively coarse knotting and the incredible colors of the central medallion suggest an older aesthetic. The three-dimensional treatment of the meandering 'T' border, though, and the manner in which it is drawn possibly indicate a fourth quarter of the 19th-century date.

Warp	: Z 2 S brown + ivory wool
Weft	: 2 sheds ivory + brown wool
Knots	: 3 + 4 ply yarn, wool
6h x 4v	= 24kpsi
Colors (5)	: dk. blue / med. blue / red / green / ivory
Size	: 71cm x 135cm (27.9in x 53.1in)

46

An old rug from Tibet with a classic running swastika border and an archaic medallion complete with a flower head in the center. The indigo blue field is beautifully dyed as is the outlining of the medallion in yellow and brown. This imparts a shining effect, with the medallion literally glowing in contrast to the dark blue field. The 'ram's horn' extensions with perfectly proportioned reciprocal forms is attractively drawn and quite archaic.

Warp	: Z 2 S ivory wool
Weft	: 1 shed ivory wool
Knots	: 4 + 5 ply yarn, wool
7h x 4v	= 28kpsi
Colors (8)	: dk. blue / med. blue / lt. blue / yellow / lavender / green / logwood / natural brown
Size	: 75cm x 142cm (29.5in x 55.9in)

■ 141

47

A beautifully colored rug exhibiting the type of medallions of which Parpola speaks with regard to the TLV mirror and mandala patterns. The endless knots floating throughout the indigo blue field are quite lovely and an extremely rare format; one does not often see this pattern used in this manner. The rug probably dates to the late 19th or early 20th century, indicated by the manner in which the meandering 'T' border is drawn as well as the floral elements in the corners of the field.

Warp	: Z 2 S ivory wool
Weft	: 2 sheds brown + gray wool
Knots	: 3 + 4 ply yarn, wool
7h x 6v	= 42kpsi
Colors (8)	: dk. blue / med. blue / blue-green / red / lt. blue / yellow / lavender / ivory
Size	: 69cm x 137cm (27.1in x 53.9in)

■ 143

48

An extremely attractive and colorful lattice pattern. Given the borders and the rather condensed treatment of the field design, it is likely this is a late 19th- or early 20th-century weaving. The diversity of the palette is unusual and quite attractive, providing an opportunity for accomplished dyers to exhibit their expertise.

Warp	: Z 2 S ivory wool
Weft	: 2 sheds red wool
Knots	: 4 + 5 ply yarn, wool
10h x 8v	= 80kpsi
Colors (8)	: dk. blue / lt. blue / red / violet / blue-green / salmon / brown / ivory
Size	: 67cm x 152cm (26.3in x 59.8in)

49

No collection of Tibetan rugs would be complete without an example of this design type. Commonly referred to as the 'frogs foot' design, this particular motif probably represents a tree pattern and is possibly symbolic of the 'tree of life' theme that appears in rugs throughout Central Asia. Stylized versions of this motif date to as early as 2000 BCE and can be seen in the engraved stone seals excavated from BMAC sites in the Gonor Oasis. This is probably a late 19th-century rug, with a simple border system and all natural dyes.

Warp	: Z 2 S ivory wool
Weft	: 1 shed ivory wool
Knots	: 3 + 4 ply yarn, wool
7h x 5.5v	= 38.5kpsi
Colors (4)	: dk. blue / med. blue / ivory / coral
Size	: 81cm x 152cm (31.8in x 59.8in)

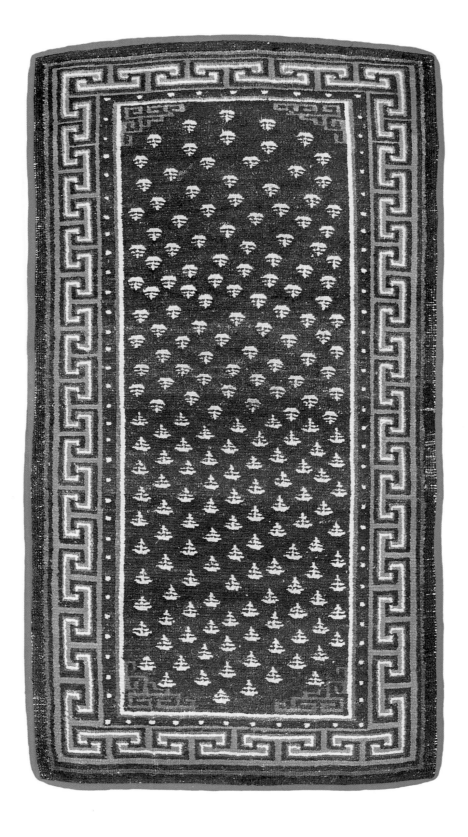

50

A lovely rug with a rare field pattern composed of the so-called 'rice grain' motif on which a classic medallion comfortably rests. This overall field pattern is possibly based on a 'tile' design prototype as it can be read in more than one way—either as octagons or 'X' forms as delineated by the yellow and brown 'grains.' The central medallion depicts the classic themes one expects to see in Tibetan weavings, with the suggestion of T-shaped corridors in the four cardinal directions which emulate the classic mandala/*stupa* prototype. The meandering 'T' border is nicely drawn and executed in a style consistent with late 19th-century dating.

Warp	: Z 2 S ivory wool
Weft	: 1 shed ivory + brown wool
Knots	: 3 ply yarn, wool
6h x 4v	= 24kpsi
Colors (7)	: red / walnut brown / yellow / dk. blue / lt. blue / lavender / ivory
Size	: 74cm x 138cm (29.1in x 54.3in)

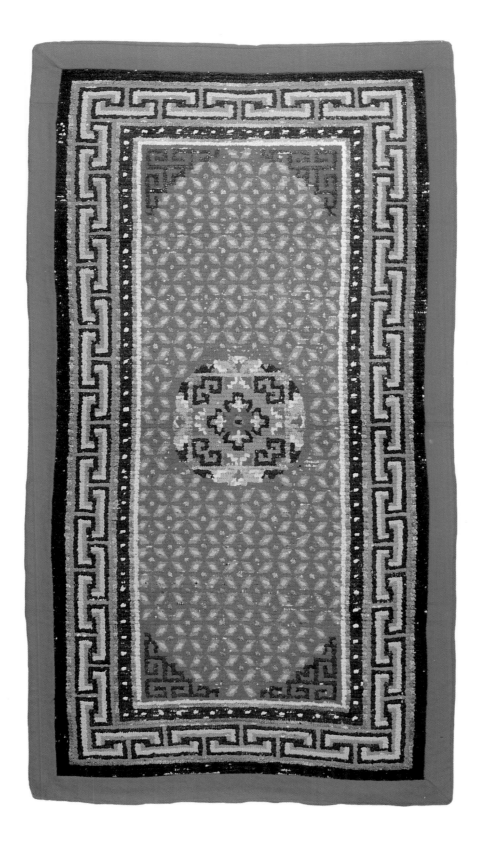

51

A lovely composition with an unusual medallion on a beautifully colored green field. The spacious free floating image is accentuated by the liquid field color, achieved by the use of a subtle and elegant abrash. The atypical medallion form is distinguished by the talismanic cross (abbreviated *vajra* ornament) in the center. The bats and clouds floating on the field are attractive features, gracefully drawn and spaciously rendered. The clouds are woven in an atypically fine manner with lovely tendril-like extensions.

Warp	: 2 ply cotton
Weft	: 1 shed gray brown wool
Knots	: 7 + 8 ply yarn, wool
6h x 4v	= 24kpsi
Colors (10)	: green / lt. green / red / lavender / lemon yellow / lt. walnut brown / lt. purple / dk. blue / lt. blue / ivory
Size	: 70cm x 151cm (27.5in x 59.4in)

52

A typical runner from Tibet intended for monastic use. The division of the design suggests separate seating for individual monks in a monastery hall. Composed of all natural dyes, the brown dye seen in the border is probably derived from walnut husk. Again, this medallion design is reminiscent of the mandalas of which Parpola writes. Probably dating to the late 19th century, the archaic treatment of the border is reminiscent of those seen in older saddle rugs.

Warp	: Z 2 S ivory wool
Weft	: 1 shed ivory wool
Knots	: 4 ply yarn, wool
6h x 4v	= 24kpsi
Colors (8)	: red / walnut brown / dk. blue / med. blue / yellow / blue-green / dk. brown overdyed with blue / ivory
Size	: 82cm x 472cm (32.2in x 185.8in)

53

Clearly a runner intended for monastic use, the deep orange ground color is closely associated with the lamas and monks of Tibet. The medallions are typical of the type seen in rugs made after 1900. The classic 'pearl' minor border separates the orange field from an interesting floral primary border. Published analogy, Kuløy, Plate 105

Warp	:	blue wool S spun
Weft	:	2 sheds brown + some blue wool
Knots	:	3, 4 + 5 ply yarn, wool
5h x 4v	=	20kpsi
Colors (10)	:	orange / red / dk. blue / pink / logwood (faded) / yellow / ivory / green / brown overdyed with blue / burgundy
Size	:	61cm x 251cm (24in x 98.8in)

54

A classic 3-medallion rug which adheres to the patterns noted by Bidder. The central medallion receives a different treatment, in this case a different color. Bidder maintains that this use of the 3-medallion format is derived from ancient Buddhist art, where the central medallion signifies a seat for the Buddha as he is flanked by an attendant on either side. The border of this rug is also unusual, utilizing a truncated lattice design usually reserved for use in the field of rugs. This creates the sinuous lines that run throughout the border, contributing to a sense of movement.

Warp	: Z 2 S ivory wool
Weft	: 1 shed ivory wool
Knots	: 3, 4 + 5 ply yarn, wool
11h x 5v	= 55kpsi
Colors (11)	: red / dk. blue / med. blue / yellow / lt. green / walnut brown / green / lt. blue / olive / gray brown / tan
Size	: 78cm x 158cm (30.7in x 62.2in)

55

The combination of medallions placed on an abstract tiger-striped field is very unusual. With the fringe on the sides, undoubtedly this rug was made as a special sleeping rug or *khaden*. Though not an exceptionally early example, the composition is very pleasing and all the colors are derived from natural dyes. The abrashed brown field is probably dyed with walnut husks.

Warp	: Z 2 S ivory wool
Weft	: 1 shed gray brown wool
Knots	: 3, 4 + 5 ply yarn, wool
8h x 4.5v	= 36kpsi
Colors (11)	: walnut brown abrash / dk. blue / med. blue / lt. blue / lt. orange / coral red / brownish maroon / ivory / pink (faded) / violet maroon / lt. blue-green
Size	: 72cm x 133cm (28.3in x 52.3in) — excludes fringe

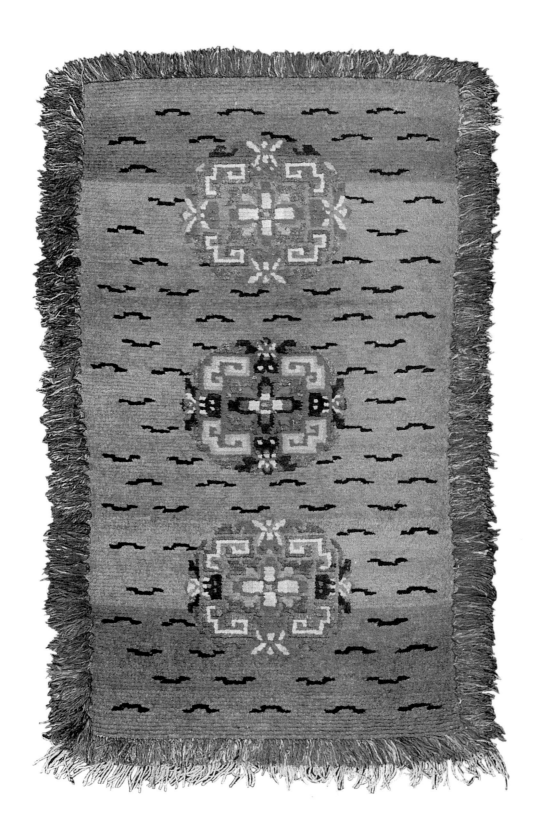

56

Another monastic rug mirroring the aesthetic seen in Plate 2, except that this has a veritable wealth of Buddhist symbols added to the 3-medallion format. The medallions are simple, with lotus flowers contained within each roundel. Again, four swastikas in alternating direction adorn the four corners of the field.

Warp	: Z 2 S ivory wool
Weft	: 1 shed brown wool
Knots	: 3 ply yarn, wool
7h x 5v	= 35kpsi
Colors (2)	: coral red / lt. green
Size	: 81cm x 153cm (31.8in x 60.2in)

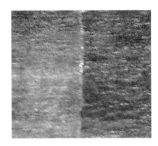

57

Woven in four strips on a narrow back strap loom, such rugs known as 'tsutruk' are probably the survivors of a nearly lost tradition of early nomadic weaving. As design is clearly not an indicator of age or beauty, only the colors used distinguish this example from others of the type. The beautifully abrashed green/blue-green field is extraordinary. The red pile 'border' may have been woven to simulate the traditional red cloth used to protect the selvedges and ends seen in many rugs from the plateau.

Warp	: Z 2 S ivory wool
Weft	: 2 sheds ivory wool
Knots	: 2 + 3 ply yarn, wool
7h x 8v	= 56kpsi
Colors (2)	: blue-green abrash / red
Size	: 69cm x 164cm (27.1in x 64.5in)

58

Another 'tsutruk', the archaic type of weaving executed on small back strap looms. Woven in three strips and sumptuously dyed with indigo, such weavings become an exercise in appreciation of a modern art aesthetic as it manifests itself in antique tribal art. The red pile surrounding the blue field, again, mimics the red cloth one often finds attached to the edges of Tibetan rugs as they are used in situ.

Warp	: Z 2 S gray wool
Weft	: 2 sheds ivory wool
Knots	: 2 ply yarn, wool
6h x 5v	= 30kpsi
Colors (2)	: red / blue
Size	: 74cm x 161cm (29.1in x 63.3in)

59

A complete saddle set with the classic notch on both of the lower corners of the larger rug, a more commonly encountered style. The central medallion is an interesting variant of a familiar type. Seen as a reciprocal pattern drawn in dark indigo blue, a floral or plant life form is depicted. The use of reciprocal patterning is not really an element in most designs seen in Tibetan rugs, and to see it used so artfully here is quite pleasing. Also note the four arrows in dark blue entering the medallion from the four cardinal directions; this is a theme consistent with Parpola's musings on the mandala/*stupa* relationship.

Warp	: Z 2 S ivory wool
Weft	: 1 shed ivory wool
Knots	: 3 ply yarn, wool
11h x 7v	= 77kpsi
Colors (11)	: lt. walnut brown / dk. blue / med. blue / lt. blue / red / orange / lt. pink / lt. coral red / burnt sienna / ivory / lt. tan
Size	: (1) 126cm x 61cm (49.6in x 24in) — excludes edging
	(2) 72cm x 55cm (28.3in x 21.6in) — excludes edging

60

An example of the so-called 'butterfly'-shaped saddle rug, designed to be placed under a saddle. Supposedly patterned after the cut of British saddle rugs, it is thought this format only became popular after the Younghusband expedition of 1904. The bats are exceptionally well drawn, detailed and animated. The foliate tendril patterns are exceptionally articulated and elegantly proportioned. As with most saddle rugs, it is woven in two sections and sewn together down the middle. Published analogy, Kuløy, Plate 96

Warp	: 5 + 6 ply cotton
Weft	: 1 shed ivory + brown wool
Knots	: 3 + 4 ply yarn, wool
10h x 6v	= 60kpsi
Colors (8)	: tan / dk. blue / lt. blue / yellow / pink / orange / red / maroon (faded)
Size	: 111cm x 66cm (44in x 26in)

61

An interesting saddle rug depicting the beloved snow lion image. Intended to be viewed from either side as it is draped over the animal, the snow lions are drawn with their backs to each other. Woven in two separate sections and subsequently sewn together down the middle, the direction in which the pile lies is identical when viewed from either side. Interestingly, the border consists of the dragon/ phoenix motifs—a rare design for a border—as well as a multi-colored 'pearl' minor border. Published analogy, Kuløy, Plate 182

Warp	: Z 2 S ivory wool
Weft	: 1 shed lt. brown wool
Knots	: 4 + 5 ply yarn, wool
10h x 5v	= 50kpsi
Colors (8)	: dk. blue / lt. blue / med. blue / red / pink / orange / ivory / violet (faded)
Size	: 109cm x 62cm (42.9in x 24.4in)

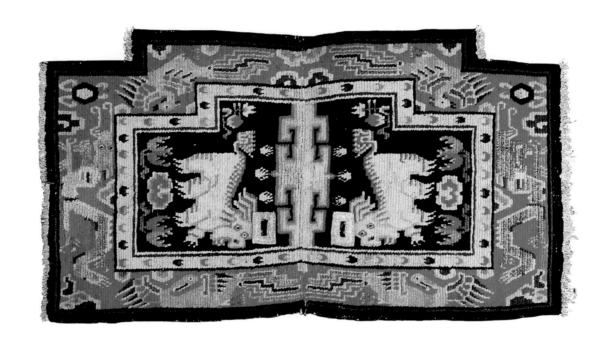

62

An interesting saddle rug from the early 20th century. Dyed only with indigo of varying strength, the composition is at once simple and elegant. Foliate plant forms with prominent flower heads are the primary pattern. But the pattern outlined in the center of the rug is an exceptionally nice and unusual feature, one that is reminiscent of a Central Asian aesthetic.

Warp	: Z 2 S ivory wool
Weft	: 2 sheds brown wool, S spun
Knots	: 2 + 3 ply yarn, wool
9h x 6v	= 54kpsi
Colors (3)	: dk. blue / lt. blue / ivory
Size	: 114cm x 71cm (44.8in x 27.9in)

63

An incredibly ornate and posh horse cover. The designs on such weavings are often drawn in this way; when the rug is draped over the back of the animal, the opposing images can be seen from either side. Classical Tibetan versions of familiar themes are seen here, including the phoenix holding a lotus flower in the beak, mountain borders on three sides and a beautifully ornate top border with scrolling vines, tendrils and flowers. The orange ground color may indicate monastic patronage. Published analogy, Kuløy, Plate 233

Warp	: Z 2 S blue + ivory wool
Weft	: 2 sheds ivory wool
Knots	: 3 ply yarn, wool
13h x 7v	= 91kpsi
Colors (11)	: orange / dk. blue / lt. blue / lt. green / lt. yellow / blue-green / red / purple (faded) / ivory pink / brownish maroon / burnt sienna
Size	: 136cm x 116cm (53.5in x 45.6in)

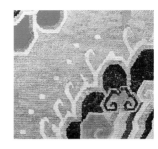

64

A beautifully designed horse cover drawn on a very large scale. Depicting flowering plants with a nicely articulated wave element in the bottom right and left corners, the light sea blue/green ground color truly imparts the idea of a verdant, fertile body of water from which these lotus flowers emerge.

Warp	: Z 2 S ivory wool
Weft	: 2 sheds ivory wool
Knots	: 4 ply yarn, wool
7h x 5v	= 35kpsi
Colors (10)	: blue-green abrash / red / dk. blue / yellow / mustard yellow / lt. orange / aubergine / raspberry / lt. blue / lt. pink
Size	: 154cm x 92cm (60.6in x 36.2in)

65

Pure graphic appeal makes this a very compelling image. With nicely drawn dragons cavorting in clouds adorning the bottom corners, the V-shaped orientation of the geometric lattice is a very strong image. Such bold graphics, best appreciated from a distance, are seldom seen in Tibetan weavings. But clearly, the patterns on this horse cover suggest it was important that the rider of the animal on which this cover was placed should be noticed. Again, the orange ground color on the corner motifs suggest a possible monastic use or patronage. Published analogy, Textile Museum Catalogue, Plate 55

Warp	: Z 2 S ivory wool
Weft	: 2 sheds lt. tan wool
Knots	: 3 + 4 ply yarn, wool
11h x 7v	= 77kpsi
Colors (10)	: orange / lt. yellow / dk. blue / lt. blue / lt. brown / red / lt. pink / blue-green / brownish maroon / ivory
Size	: 145cm x 83cm (57in x 32.6in)

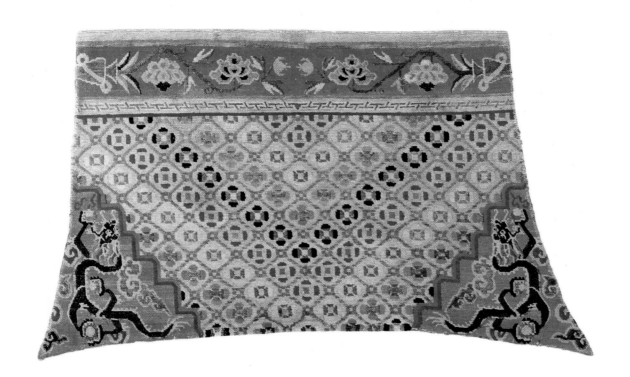

66

An unusually patterned horse blanket lacking the overall monastic palette that would suggest ecclesiastic use. The elements within the lattice, reminiscent of the Turkmen 'erre' *gol*, are arranged in diagonal rows defined by the use of color with an understated 'wave' or water pattern in either of the lower corners. The colors appear to be all natural dyes and the cover probably dates to the fourth quarter of the 19th century.

Warp	: Z 2 S ivory + gray wool
Weft	: 2 sheds gray brown wool
Knots	: 5 ply yarn, wool
8h x 4v	= 32kpsi
Colors (9)	: dk. blue / lt. blue / ivory / red / lt. orange (faded) / purple (faded) / burnt sienna (slightly faded) / khaki tan / lt. red
Size	: 138cm x 87cm (54.3in x 34.2in)

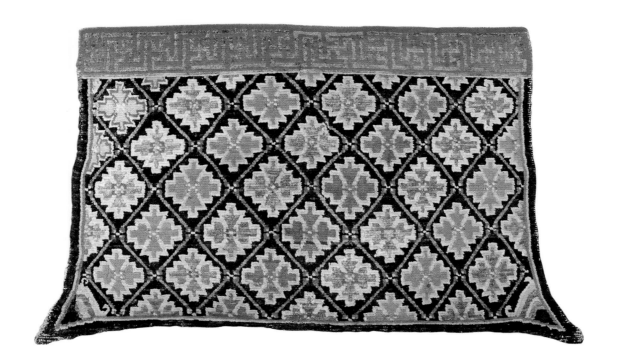

67

An early 20th-century horse blanket with a very large scale and attractive design. The finely articulated water/wave pattern in the corners with droplets of water thrown into the air by the surging tide is reminiscent of those seen in earlier Qing period textiles. Interestingly, the weaver chose to depict the vase and flowering plant motif in the top end border; this is a motif more common in weavings from the oasis weaving centers of Xinjiang. The rounded bodies of the vases reflects an older aesthetic associated with 18th-century weavings from that area.

Warp	: Z 2 S ivory wool
Weft	: 1 shed ivory wool
Knots	: 5 ply yarn, wool
9h x 4.5v	= 40.5kpsi
Colors (8)	: dk. blue / lt. blue / red / pink (faded) / purple / lt. orange / khaki tan / ivory
Size	: 142cm x 90cm (55.9in x 35.4in)

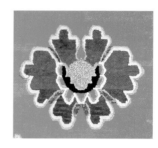

68

A boldly drawn pattern consisting of large flower heads arranged on an orange/gold ground color. The chrysanthemum forms are elegantly colored with an aubergine hue that is quite attractive. The bold simplicity of patterning with minimal ornamentation is quite attractive and is designed to be appreciated from a distance. The orange hues again suggest monastic patronage.

Warp	: 5 ply cotton
Weft	: 2 ply wool
Knots	: 5 ply yarn, wool
10h x 6v	= 60kpsi
Colors (10)	: orange / gold / red / dk. blue / med. blue / lt. blue / ivory / lt. pink / med. aubergine / pink
Size	: 162cm x 114cm (63.7in x 44.8in)

Bibliography

Barber, Elizabeth W. *The Mummies of Urumchi*. Macmillan Publishers, UK, 2000

Basilov, Vladimir N and Zhukovskaya, Natalya L. "Religious Beliefs" in *Nomads of Eurasia*. Edited by Vladimir Basilov. Seattle: University of Washington, 1989

Beckwith, Christopher I. *The Tibetan Empire in Central Asia*. Princeton University Press, 1987

Bedi, Ramesh and Bedi, Rajesh. *Ladakh—The Trans Himalayan Kingdom*. Roli Books International, New Delhi, 1981

Bell, Charles. *The People of Tibet*. Oxford Clarendon Press, 1928. Asian Educational Services, New Delhi and Madras. Re-printed 1991

Bower, Hamilton. *Diary of a Journey Across Tibet*. Ratna Phustok Press, 1894. Re-printed 1976

Christie, Anthony. *Chinese Mythology*. Hamlyn Publishing Group, Rushden UK, 1983

Cole, Thomas. *A Tribal Tradition*. HALI #49, February 1990

Cole, Thomas. *Chinese Rugs—Art from the Steppes*. HALI #67, February/March 1993

Cole, Thomas. *Commentary on Tibetan Rugs*. Arts of Asia, May–June 1990

Cole, Thomas. *In The Plateau Style*. HALI #131, December 2003

Contemporaries of Marco Polo. Edited by Manuel Komroff. Dorset Press, New York, 1989

Das, Sarat Chandra. *Journey to Lhasa and Central Tibet*. 1902. Edited by W. W. Rockhill. Re-printed by Cosmo Publications, 1988

Eiland, Murray, Jr. *Chinese and Exotic Rugs*. New York Graphic Society, Boston, 1979

Eiland, Murray, Jr. *Tibetan Rugs at Adraskand*. Oriental Rug Review, Vol. 11, #6

Fiero, Gloria. *The Humanistic Tradition*. McGraw-Hill, New York, 2002

Frankfort, H. P. *The Central Asian Dimension of the Symbolic System in Bactria and Margiana*. June, 1994 Antiquities, Vol. 68, #259, Oxford University Press

Gantzhorn, Volkmar. *The Oriental Carpet—A Presentation of its Development, Iconologically and*

Iconographically, from its Beginnings to the 18th Century. Benedikt Taschen Verlag Gmbrl & Co., Germany, 1991

Grousset, René. *The Empire of the Steppes—A History of Central Asia*. Translated by Naomi Walford. Rutgers University Press, New Brunswick, New Jersey, 1970

Hiebert, Fredrik. *Production Evidence for the Origins of the Oxus Civilisation*. June, 1994 Antiquities, Vol. 68, #259, Oxford University Press

Holdich, Thomas. *Tibet The Mysterious*. Asian Educational Services, 1906. New Delhi and Madras. Re-printed 1996

Huber, Christoph. *Old Motifs*. Ghereh #22, Winter 1999/2000

Krotkov, Jasmine. *Tibetan Rug Design in History*. Oriental Rug Review, Vol. 11, #2

Kuløy, Hallvard Kåre. *Tibetan Rugs*. White Orchid Press, Bangkok, 1982

Kuznetsov, B. I. *Influence of the Pamirs on Tibetan Culture*. Tibet Journal, Autumn 1978

Lindahl, David and Knorr, Thomas. *Uzbek*. Zbinden Druck & Verlag AG, Basel, 1975

Masson, V. M. *"Seals of a Proto-Indian Type from Altyn-Depe"*, the Bronze Age Civilisation of Central Asia. Ed. Philip L. Kohl and M. E. Sharpe. Armonk, New York, 1981

Mellart, James. *Excavations at Hacilar, Vol. 2*. Edinburgh University Press for British Institute of Archaeology

Myers, Diana K. *Temple, Household, Horseback—Rugs of the Tibetan Plateau*. The Textile Museum, Washington DC, 1984

Namkhai Norbhu. *Tibetan Culture*. Tibet Journal, Autumn 1978

Narratives of the Mission of George Bogle to Tibet and of the Journey of Thomas Manning to Lhasa. Edited by Clements R. Markham. First published 1876. Genesis Publishing Pte. Ltd., 1989

Parker, E. H. *A Thousand Years of the Tartars*. Dorset Press, New York, 1987

Parpola, Asko. *Pre-Proto-Iranians of Afghanistan as Initiators of Sakta Tantricism on the Scything/Sakta Affiliations of the Dasas, Nuristanis and Magadians*. Iranian Antique–Vol.XXXVII, Helsinki, 2002

P'Yankova, L. *Central Asia in the Bronze Age: Sedentary and Nomadic Cultures.* June, 1994 Antiquities, Vol. 68, #259, Oxford University Press

Rice, Tamara Talbot. *Ancient Arts of Central Asia.* Frederick A. Praeger, New York/Washington, 1965

Rinchen Lhamo. *We Tibetans.* Original 1926, London. Srishti Publishers & Distributors, New Delhi, 1997

Rockhill, William Woodville. *The Land of the Lamas.* 1891, London, Longmans, Green, and Co., Asian Educational Services, New Delhi and Madras. Re-printed 1988

Roerich, J. N. *The Animal Style Among the Nomad Tribes of Northern Tibet.* Seminarium Kondakovianum, Prague, 1930

Rossabi, M. *Kublai Khan.* UC Press, Berkeley–Los Angeles–London, 1984

Rudenko, Sergei. *Frozen Tombs of Siberia—The Pazyryk Burials of Iron Age Horsemen.* California Press, Berkeley–Los Angeles, 1970

Sassouni, Viken. *Armenian Church Floor Plan—a hitherto unidentified design in Oriental Rugs.* HALI Vol. 4, #1

Shaw, Miranda. *Passionate Enlightenment: Women in Tantric Buddhism.* Princeton University, Princeton, New Jersey, 1994

Singer, Jane Casey. "The Cultural Roots of Early Central Tibetan Painting" in *Sacred Visions: Early Paintings from Central Tibet.* Edited by Steven M. Kossak and Jane Casey Singer. Harry N. Abrams, New York, 1998

Stein, R. A. *Tibetan Civilization.* Stanford University, 1970

Travels in Tartary, Thibet, and China 1844–1846. Huc and Gabet. Translated by William Halitt. Asian Educational Services, New Delhi and Madras, 1988

Tseh-ring-thar. *The Ancient Zhang-Zhung Civilization.* Tibet Studies, June 1989

Tung, Rosemary Jones. *A Portrait of Lost Tibet.* Photographs by Ilya Tolstoy and Brooke Dolan. Thames and Hudson (UK only), 1980

Turkmen—Tribal Carpets and Traditions. Edited by Louise Mackie and Jon Thompson. The Textile Museum, Washington DC, 1980

Wright, Nicholas. *Tibetan Rugs—Chinese But With a Difference.* Oriental Rug Review, Vol. 9, #4